Lewis Thomas

By Andrew J. Angyal

Elon College

Twayne Publishers
A Division of G. K. Hall & Co. • Boston

Lewis Thomas
Andrew J. Angyal

Copyediting supervised by Barbara Sutton
Book production by Janet Z. Reynolds
Book design by Barbara Anderson

Typeset in 11 pt. Garamond
by Williams Press, Inc., Albany, New York

Printed on permanent/durable acid-free paper
and bound in the United States of America

Library of Congress Cataloging-in-Publication Data
Angyal, Andrew J.
  Lewis Thomas.

  (Twayne's United States authors series; TUSAS 547)
  Bibliography: p.
  Includes index.
  1. Thomas, Lewis, 1913–   —Criticism and inter-
pretation.   2. Literature and science—United States.
3. Literature and medicine.   I. Title.   II. Series.
PS3570.H566Z54   1989   814'.54   88–34761
ISBN 0–8057–7536–6

For Jeffrey and Evan

Contents

About the Author

The relationship between science and literature has long interested Andrew J. Angyal. The author of a Twayne biography of Loren Eiseley, Angyal has also published a number of book reviews and articles on contemporary science writers. He is an associate professor of English at Elon College, where he has taught for the past twelve years. His degrees include a B.A. in English from Queens College of the City University of New York, a M.A.R. from Yale Divinity School, and a Ph.D. in English from Duke University. Angyal has been appointed a visiting Fulbright lecturer in American literature at Louis Kossuth University in Debrecen, Hungary, and has taught American literature at Adam Mickiewicz University in Poznan, Poland. He has also served as a PICA (Piedmont Independent College Association) visiting fellow at Guilford College. His interest in Lewis Thomas stems back to the publication of Thomas's first collection of essays, *The Lives of a Cell,* in 1974. Angyal has lectured on Dr. Thomas and other American science writers during his Fulbright appointment in Hungary. He has also written the introduction to the forthcoming Hungarian edition of Thomas's *Lives of a Cell.*

Preface

Lewis Thomas's essays have been included in virtually every freshman English anthology, yet surprisingly little critical attention has been paid to his writing, despite the growing interest in nonfiction prose and rhetorical forms. As a medical researcher and administrator, Dr. Thomas is highly respected within his field, yet through the personal-essay form he has also reached a wide public and academic audience. As a scientist, writing about the implications of science for contemporary culture, he has made effective use of the reflective and exploratory forms of the familiar essay.

Organicism is the root metaphor in all of Thomas's writing. He believes that the earth's biosphere is one large, integrated whole and that the human community is an integral part of that whole, perhaps a kind of global nervous system. Symbiosis and altruism, not just competition, are the driving forces behind this universe, and Thomas believes that humans should consciously aspire to the harmony and altruistic cooperation evident everywhere in nature. Models of biological cooperation are evident everywhere, from the complex ecology of the cell to the intricate social behavior of bees and ants to the strange symbiotic relationships apparent among many marine animals, such as his famous example of the medusa and the snail. Partnerships are essential in nature, where everything is alive thanks to something else. Nothing exists absolutely alone and independent. Not all symbiotic relationships are benign, however, since the anomaly of illness often results from inconclusive or flawed negotiations between host and parasite. Human disease can be viewed as an overstepping of the bounds, a biological misinterpretation of borders. The ultimate image of organicism, of course, is the planet earth itself, conceived by Thomas as a gigantic living cell, elaborately organized and self-contained, self-regulating, surrounded by a huge membrane, capable of maintaining its internal equilibrium by capturing and storing the energy of the sun and slowly releasing it to living organisms. From space it resembles a huge embryo.

Like it or not, humans are an integral part of this global ecosystem, and our use of language may be the biological mechanism that most closely links us together. In *The Lives of a Cell,* Thomas presents himself as a harbinger of good news in a gloomy age. We are not solitary, isolated creatures but are embedded in nature as an integral part of the global ecosystem. Thomas's organicism shapes his view of human nature as well. He is a meliorist who strongly believes in the value of basic scientific research as a corrective to pessimism and ignorance. Our major problem is "our profound ignorance of nature." Fortuitous error is the driving force of both genetic change and human thought. This capacity to err is built into the fabric of human language through a wonderful imprecision that permits fresh and original thought. The greatest human triumph, according to Thomas, is found in the harmonious structure of classical music, particularly the music of Johann Sebastian Bach, whose compositions mirror the transformation of inanimate matter into the ordered dance of living forms.

Thomas's root metaphor of organicism points to many interesting possibilities of collaboration between the sciences and the humanities. His insistence on our talent for language as both the mark of our human uniqueness and the expression of our social identity grows out of a personal conviction that human beings are generally predisposed to cooperate. Communication through language is both the medium and the expression of our social nature. Thomas's belief in the efficacy of scientific research as a model of human cooperation derives from the same root metaphor. He perceives his administrative work as yet another form of collaborative behavior, assisting others to work toward institutional goals, and thus his scientific outlook, his writing, and his concept of himself as a leader all share the same coherent philosophy.

Since Thomas's career as an essayist did not begin until he was in his fifties, in 1970, this book follows a somewhat different plan than most of the titles in this series. The first two chapters are devoted to an account of Dr. Thomas's earlier years as a medical student and then as a distinguished medical researcher. These chapters include descriptions of his early humorous writing for the *Princeton Tiger* and of his poetry, evidencing literary interests that a busy career did not permit him to pursue. Chapters 3 and 4 then examine the essays he published while continuing his career as biomedical researcher and administrator at a number of prominent medical institutions. My discussion of Thomas's essays is thematically organized in terms of the principal subjects and issues that have engrossed him. I offer some assessment of Thomas's significance as a contemporary essayist and prose stylist and consider his influence on the resurgence of interest in the essay genre and in the growing field of scientific and medical writing for the general reader.

Perhaps Thomas's most important literary accomplishment has been his ability to reach out to a broad public audience, using the familiar essay to articulate his unique personal vision. His success has been an inspiration to other physicians and medical scientists, notably Gerald Weissman, Oliver Sacks, Richard Selzer, Melvin Konner, Perri Klass, and others, to maintain the tradition of medical humanism in an age of overspecialization.

Andrew J. Angyal

Elon College

Acknowledgments

This book would not have been possible without the encouragement and cooperation of Dr. Lewis Thomas. Not only was he kind enough to grant his permission to undertake this study, but he and Stephanie Hemmert, his secretary, at the Memorial Sloan-Kettering Cancer Institute, have patiently answered numerous queries. I am also grateful to Dr. Thomas for agreeing to be interviewed during the summer of 1985, while I was researching this book, and for permitting me to quote from his essays, articles, and poems.

Many of Dr. Thomas's friends and colleagues agreed to be interviewed or otherwise offered their assistance. My special thanks to Dr. H. Sherwood Lawrence, New York University School of Medicine; Dr. Floyd Denny, University of North Carolina School of Medicine; Dr. Wallace A. Clyde, Jr., UNC School of Medicine; Dr. Eugene Stead, Duke University Medical Center; Dr. Saul J. Farber, Dean, NYU School of Medicine; Dr. Martin S. Begun, Associate Dean, NYU School of Medicine; Dr. Edward A. Boyce, Memorial Sloan-Kettering; and others as well.

My thanks for the patience and courtesy of a number of librarians and archivists, especially Nicholas Falco, curator, Queensboro Public Library, and Earle E. Coleman, Princeton University archivist.

Additional assistance was provided by Lawrence N. Tallamy, acting headmaster of the McBurney School, and Dr. James Gifford, Duke University medical historian.

A series of summer grants from Elon College helped defray travel and research expenses. The staff of McEwen Library offered their kind assistance on countless occasions. A number of colleagues and friends were gracious enough to read and offer their comments. My special thanks to Russell Gill and John Herold. Dr. James Patterson was kind enough to read my manuscript for medical inaccuracies: any remaining errors are my own responsibility. To my wife, Jennifer, who read and discussed every chapter with me, I owe a special debt of gratitude. And to my sons, Jeffrey and Evan, who grew with this book as it grew, I dedicate these efforts.

For permission to quote copyrighted material from Lewis Thomas's published work, my thanks are extended to Viking Penguin, Inc.: (1) From *The Lives of a Cell* by Lewis Thomas. © 1971, 1972, 1973 by the Massachusetts Medical Society. © 1974 by Lewis Thomas. Originally published in the *New England Journal of Medicine*.* (2) From *The Medusa and the Snail* by Lewis Thomas. © 1974, 1975, 1976, 1977, 1978, 1979 by Lewis Thomas. Originally published in the *New England Journal of Medicine*.* (3) From *The Youngest Science* by Lewis Thomas. © 1983 by Lewis Thomas.* (4) From *Late Night Thoughts on Listening to Mahler's Ninth Symphony* by Lewis Thomas. © 1980, 1981, 1982, 1983 by Lewis Thomas.*
* Reprinted by permission of Viking Penguin, Inc.

Chronology

1913   Lewis Thomas born, 25 November, in Flushing, New York, the fourth of five children of Dr. Joseph S. Thomas and Grace (Peck) Thomas.

1918   Enters P.S. 20, Flushing.

1926   Attends Flushing High School for three semesters.

1927   Enters the McBurney School in Manhattan, in September.

1929   Graduates from the McBurney School and enters Princeton at the age of fifteen.

1933   Graduates from Princeton with B.S. in biology. Enters Harvard Medical School at the age of nineteen.

1937   Graduates from Harvard Medical School, cum laude.

1937–1939   Serves internship on Fourth (Harvard) Service, Boston City Hospital.

1939–1941   Completes residency at the Neurological Institute, Columbia Presbyterian Medical Center.

1941   Marries Beryl Dawson in Manhattan on 1 January. Goes to Halifax, Nova Scotia, to treat meningitis outbreak. Returns to Boston as research fellow at Thorndike Memorial Laboratory. Daughter Abigail born 13 October.

1942–1943   Commissioned as a lieutenant in U.S. Naval Reserve. Assigned to Naval Medical Research Unit no. 1 at Rockefeller Institute in New York.

1944   Completes basic training at San Bruno, California. Daughter Judith born 6 March.

1944–1945   Stationed in Guam and Okinawa as a virologist.

1946   Discharged from navy as a lieutenant commander.

1946–1948   Assistant professor of pediatrics at Johns Hopkins University Medical School in Baltimore. Daughter Eliza born 4 April 1948.

1948–1949   Associate professor of medicine and director of the Division of Infectious Disease at Tulane University School of Medicine in New Orleans.

1949–1950   Promoted to professor of medicine at Tulane.

1950–1954   Professor of pediatrics and internal medicine; and American Legion Heart Professor, University of Minnesota Medical School in Minneapolis.

1954–1958   Professor and chairman of Department of Pathology at the New York University–Bellevue Medical Center.

1957–1969   Member of the New York City Board of Health.

1958–1966   Professor and chairman of the Department of Medicine at NYU–Bellevue Medical Center. Director of third and fourth medical divisions, Bellevue Hospital.

1959–1966   Director of medicine, University Hospital.

1961–1963   Chairman of Narcotics Advisory Committee of the New York City Health Research Council.

1963–1965   President of the Medical Board of Bellevue Hospital.

1966–1969   Dean of the New York University School of Medicine and deputy director of its Medical Center.

1969–1972   Professor and chairman of Department of Pathology at Yale–New Haven Medical Center. Chief of pathology, Yale–New Haven Hospital.

1970   Dr. Franz Ingelfinger, editor of *New England Journal of Medicine,* invites Thomas to contribute a monthly column, "Notes of a Biology Watcher," which he continues from 1971 to 1980.

1972   Appointed dean of Yale University School of Medicine.

1973–1980   Appointed president and chief executive officer of the Memorial Sloan-Kettering Cancer Center in Manhattan.

1974   *The Lives of a Cell.* Wins National Book Award, 1975. Earns first honorary degree from University of Rochester.

1977–1978   Phi Beta Kappa visiting scholar at Harvard.

1979   *The Medusa and the Snail.* Wins Christopher Award.

1980   Woodrow Wilson Award, Princeton University. Award in literature, American Academy and Institute of Arts and Letters.

1980–1983   Chancellor of the Memorial Sloan-Kettering Cancer Center. Begins columns for *Discover* magazine.

1983   *The Youngest Science* (memoir) and *Late Night Thoughts on Listening to Mahler's Ninth Symphony*. Named president emeritus, Memorial Sloan-Kettering Cancer Center. Kober Medal, Association of American Physicians.

1984   Appointed university professor, SUNY–Stony Brook. Member, American Academy and Institute of Arts and Letters. Public Service Award, the Harvard School of Public Health.

1985   *Could I Ask You Something?* (poetry).

1986   Lewis Thomas Award for Communications, American College of Physicians. Britannica Award, *Encyclopedia Britannica*. Dedication of the Lewis Thomas Laboratory, Princeton University.

1987   Alfred P. Sloan, Jr., Memorial Award, American Cancer Society.

1988   President-elect, New York Academy of Sciences.

Chapter One

The Making of a Physician

Lewis Thomas takes his place among an eminent group of physicians who have found time in their busy practices to devote themselves to letters as well. Perhaps the combination of precise diagnostic training and clinical detachment enables the physician to succeed as a writer, for there has been a long tradition of authors—Sir Thomas Browne, Oliver Goldsmith, Tobias Smollett, John Keats, Oliver Wendell Holmes, Anton Chekhov, W. Somerset Maugham, A. Conan Doyle, William Carlos Williams, Walker Percy, Oliver Sacks, and Richard Selzer, for example—who have studied or practiced medicine or surgery. The essay in particular seems to be a congenial literary form for the physician-writer because the medium itself encourages a combination of careful observation and detached reflection.

In his essays, Thomas employs a distinct style noted for its brevity and informality, its crisp factuality, dry humor, and cheerfully optimistic outlook. He often adopts the tone of an old-fashioned family physician dispensing no-nonsense advice to his readers, though he can be whimsical or philosophical as well. His credentials as a physician, cancer researcher, and medical administrator lend unquestioned authority to his essays, but it is his distinctive style and vision that have won him such high praise in reviews by Joyce Carol Oates, John Updike, and others. In fact, his first essay collection, *The Lives of a Cell* (1974), earned the unusual distinction of being nominated for a National Book Award in both the arts and the sciences.

For a writer who has demonstrated such mastery of the essay form, Thomas turned to essay writing relatively late and largely by accident. Though he "dabbled" in poetry and wrote humorous sketches as an undergraduate, he majored in biology and from college went straight to Harvard Medical School. After completing his clinical training in neurology, pathology, and immunology, he has enjoyed a brilliant career in medical research and administration, including serving as dean of Yale Medical School and as chancellor of the Sloan-Kettering Cancer Institute in New York. Though Thomas has published over two hundred articles for professional journals, he only started writing short personal essays for publication in the *New England Journal of Medicine* in 1971, at the invitation of editor Franz Ingelfinger. His monthly column there, "Notes of a Biology Watcher," attracted the interest of so many readers that Viking Press eventually contacted him about the possibility of collecting his essays in book form. The result was the publication of *The Lives of a Cell* in 1974. More recently, Thomas has also appeared as a regular columnist for *Discover* magazine and has published two subsequent essay volumes and a medical memoir, but he has retained the succinct style of his early *Journal* columns.

A Physician's Son

The son of a well-respected physician and general surgeon in Flushing, New York, Lewis Thomas came by his interest in science and medicine through family influence. His father, Dr. Joseph Simon Thomas, was born on 30 October 1877, into a merchant family in Jersey City, New Jersey, where his father ran a flour mill. The Thomases were originally hod carriers of Welsh origin who had immigrated to America several generations earlier.[1] Joseph Simon Thomas attended Princeton University, as did his two brothers, and graduated with a degree in biology in 1899. He promptly entered the College of Physicians and Surgeons at Columbia University and earned his medical degree there in 1904. After his graduation from Columbia he served his internship and residency at Roosevelt Hospital in Manhattan, a prestigious teaching hospital from which a young physician could launch a successful medical practice in the New York metropolitan area. While serving his residency at Roosevelt Hospital, Dr. Joseph Thomas met a young nurse from Connecticut, Grace Emma Peck, who was in charge of the children's ward and who later served as the personal assistant to the chief surgeon, Dr. George Brewer, when he went out to perform surgery at various Long Island estates.[2] Dr. Thomas was impressed enough by this capable young nurse to propose to her toward the end of his residency, and they were married in New York City on 31 October 1906.[3]

As Lewis Thomas recalls in his memoir, *The Youngest Science,* his mother "had been raised on a small, always impoverished farm near Beacon Falls," a small village in Connecticut between New Haven and Waterbury. There she had experienced a hard childhood. "She was orphaned at the age of five or six, raised by grandparents and several unaffectionate aunts," as Thomas recalls, in a dreary, Spartan place, from which "she fled when she could, at the age of seventeen, and boarded a boat from Bridgeport to New York." With a letter of recommendation from her family doctor, she was admitted to the nursing program at Roosevelt Hospital as "a strong-minded, intelligent girl who would make a good nurse." In 1903, she completed her studies and became a registered nurse. Thomas remembers his mother as a tall, serious-minded woman, devoted to her husband and family; she did not practice nursing after her marriage but on occasion would help her husband with medical emergencies in his office and eventually developed "an informal, unpaid practice of her own." With the help of only a maid, she raised five children and did all of the cooking, much of the cleaning in their large, Victorian house, and the gardening besides. One of Thomas's earliest memories is of his mother standing in the back yard, peering intently at the lawn. Financial worries caused by patients' unpaid bills would sometimes send her outside to hunt for four-leaf clovers, but whenever she found one, she always reassured her son that "the Lord will provide."[4]

The Village of Flushing

In 1906, Dr. Joseph Thomas and his wife decided to move to the village of Flushing, in the borough of Queens, to set up his new practice, because of the good prospects for a young doctor there. At that time Flushing was a quiet, attractive country town within easy reach of Manhattan by trolley and ferry. The village was noted for its good schools and hospital, fine old homes, beautiful estates, attractive gardens, and tree-lined streets. Although its name came from the Dutch *Vlissingen,* Flushing had a strong sense of its early Quaker heritage as the site of the John Bowne House and the signing of the Flushing Remonstrance in 1657 to guarantee religious freedom for all dissenters. In 1813, the Flushing Females Association was founded to teach runaway black girls how to read and write. During the Civil War the village served as a stop on the Underground Railroad to Canada. It was the home of Daniel Carter Beard, one of the founders of the Boy Scouts of America, and Charles Dana Gibson, creator of the famous "Gibson Girl" image, who drew his first sketches on the blackboards of the old Flushing High School.[5]

Soon after the Thomases settled in Flushing, three daughters, Nancy, Ruth, and Edith, were born between 1908 and 1911. Their son Lewis

was born on 25 November 1913, and another boy, Joseph, followed
later. With their growing family, the Thomases purchased a large, white
frame house at 259 Amity Street, on the block between Bowne and
Parson Streets, a middle-class neighborhood located near the Dutch
Reformed Church, where they became members. Behind the homes on
Amity Street were backyard gardens with shade trees and flowers.
Beyond the yards lay an embankment that led to the North Shore
Division of the Long Island Railroad. Today the white frame houses
are gone, replaced by high-rise apartments, and the street has been
renamed Roosevelt Avenue. The Dutch Reformed Church is now Korean
Protestant, and according to Thomas, little evidence remains of the
places associated with his boyhood memories.[6]

The customary practice at the time was for general practitioners to
see patients in the physicians' homes, so Dr. Joseph Thomas set up
his office on the first floor of their home, and the family lived on the
second, although their dining room was on the first floor next to the
patients' waiting room, which often meant hurried meals. Dr. Thomas
would see patients in his front parlor office, and since there was no
nurse or receptionist to show patients in, this function was performed
by family members or by the doctor himself, who would call out,
"Next please." In those days physicians worked long hours, took few
holidays, and generally earned no more than a modest income. No one
entered medicine expecting to get rich. Dr. Thomas spent much of his
day making house calls, first by bicycle, then by horse and buggy, and
later by automobile. In the winter he would even wade through snowdrifts
to see his patients, but he loved his work and once during the depression
years when a patient asked him why he was so cheerful, he replied:
"I have a reason to be cheerful. I'm working!"[7]

Dr. Thomas made his daily rounds at Flushing Hospital early in the
morning, followed by house calls, a brief lunch, office hours from one
to two, more house calls in the afternoon, dinner, and evening office
hours from seven to eight. Late in the evening the telephone would
often ring, and Lewis Thomas remembers his father getting up sleepily
to speak with a patient and leave once more on a house call.[8] In the
case of serious illnesses, a doctor couldn't do much beyond diagnose
the ailment, reassure the patient, and prescribe some harmless placebo,
but he was expected to visit the sick in their homes and to show a
good bedside manner. His job was to provide consolation and encouragement for his patients. Dr. Thomas was fond of saying that a

physician's task was "to cure sometimes, to help often, and to serve always."[9]

Dr. Joseph Thomas was a gruff but kindly man with a no-nonsense manner who was highly respected by his patients. He had a twinkle in his eye, a keen mind, a touch of Welsh temper, and a droll sense of humor. Though he was not the society doctor in Flushing, he had a large middle- and working-class practice. He knew his patients and their families well, doing everything from treating them for childhood illnesses to sitting bedside with the dying. During the 1918 flu epidemic he worked indefatigably, despite the obvious risks to himself and his family. He was a good diagnostician who could disarm his patients and observe them when they were unawares. About the value of prescriptions he was skeptical, and he would not prescribe unless he was absolutely certain that the medication would do some good. Scrupulously honest in paying his own bills, he had a flexible fee scale and would not refuse charity cases, which often put a strain on his own family budget. Though he could be brusque and impatient about patients' minor complaints, he was especially good with children and could set a frightened child's broken arm and kiss it or take a sick child in his arms and rock the child to sleep. Once when he had to remove a boy's foot because of gangrene infection, he could not tell the lad that he would never walk again, so someone else had to tell him.

In his fifties, Dr. Joseph Thomas grew weary of general practice and decided to take several years off and return to Columbia to study surgery. After completing his studies, he became a member of the American College of Surgeons. When he returned to Flushing, he limited his practice to surgery but still continued to see many of his old patients. Eventually he became surgical director at Flushing Hospital and was much in demand as a surgical consultant because of his innate skepticism and his reluctance to operate unless absolutely necessary.[10]

Early Years

Some of Lewis Thomas's earliest memories are of accompanying his father in the front seat of their family sedan while Dr. Thomas made house calls or visited patients at Flushing Hospital. Dr. Thomas secretly hoped that his sons would also become physicians, as both eventually did. He talked with Lewis about his patients and explained how little medicine could actually accomplish. With a serious illness, all a physician could do was make an accurate diagnosis and provide good recuperative care. Beyond that, the disease would take its course and the doctor could only hope for the best. Some patients recovered; others didn't. This widespread doctrine of "therapeutic nihilism" continued for another generation, until the discovery of penicillin and the other wonder drugs transformed the treatment of disease. Before the 1940s, however, medicine was still primarily a healing art, not yet a science.

On a visit to one big house on Sanford Avenue owned by a prominent Christian Scientist, Dr. Joseph Thomas had to park a block away and walk to avoid embarrassing his patient. Another tale concerned an unwanted child who was rescued from a prominent Flushing family and placed in a Catholic foundling hospital after the grandmother tried to smother it with a pillow. And there was the local Baptist minister who loudly proclaimed from the pulpit that God had healed him after Dr. Thomas had performed a difficult gallbladder operation on him. "God indeed," replied Mrs. Thomas to her children, when she read the newspaper account of the sermon. "God had nothing to do with it. It was your father."[11]

Lewis Thomas enjoyed a typical childhood for a boy of his generation. As the fourth of five children, he was no doubt closely supervised by his older sisters, and in turn he no doubt responded with the typical pranks and mischief. The kids in his neighborhood rang doorbells and hid, chalked sidewalks, rifled gumball machines, and sneaked cigarettes on the curb. He remembers watching from his bicycle as "Crazy Willie," the town garbageman, rode by on his wagon or sometimes rummaged through trash barrels. Flushing children were warned by their parents to avoid this colorful character. During the day, mothers pushed their infants in high-wheeled perambulators while older children played hoops along the tree-lined streets. At dusk, John the lamplighter performed his magic. Boys played sandlot baseball, bicycled, or cooked "mickeys" or "weenies" among the heavy coastal batteries at Fort Totten, overlooking Flushing Bay. In the summer, there was swimming or sailing at Port Washington, Roslyn Harbor, or around Whitestone.

When the time came, Lewis attended P.S. 20, the neighborhood elementary school, on the corner of Sanford Avenue and Union Street. On Wednesday afternoons he went to Miss Florence's dancing class, where he was sometimes paired with another reluctant boy when there weren't enough girls for partners. Once when he was in grammar school, he was knocked unconscious by a pitched baseball and complained the next day of a nerve injury, but his mother discovered that it was nothing more than head lice, picked up by wearing someone else's cap. He was soon deloused with kerosene, shampoo, a thorough combing, and a short haircut![12] Later he became a member of the local Boy Scout troop and marched in the Memorial Day and Fourth of July parades, even reciting the Gettysburg Address one year in front of the Flushing Civil War Memorial. Several of the fathers and sons got together a literary discussion group called the Fireside Club, which met each month at various members' homes to hear a paper, followed by discussion and a rather elaborate dinner prepared by the mothers. To test the boys one winter evening, a prominent lawyer in the group offered a fifteen-dollar prize to whoever could answer a complicated Old Testament riddle involving salt. Lewis, who was rather reserved and slightly sardonic, although generally acknowledged as the intellectual leader among the group, listened for perhaps thirty seconds and came forth with the correct answer, Lot's wife.[13]

The McBurney School

Lewis Thomas was a good enough student to skip a few grades, so he was just thirteen when he entered Flushing High School in January 1926. There he studied Latin, French, biology, civics, history, mathematics, and algebra, completing three semesters at Flushing before he transferred out in September 1927.[14] His parents, recognizing his academic ability, decided that they wanted smaller classes and better instruction for their son, so they transferred him to the McBurney School on West 63rd Street, a private, YMCA-affiliated day school in Manhattan. Once the subway came out to Flushing in the 1920s, it provided quick and inexpensive access to New York City, and Thomas's parents felt that it was worth the subway ride for him to have the advantages of a private school. Lewis had earned enough credits to enter McBurney as a junior, and he spent his last two years of high school there, graduating in 1929 when he was still only fifteen.

Thomas spent two active and productive years at the McBurney School. A superior student, he earned excellent grades in all of his courses while taking a demanding academic program with a heavy concentration in mathematics, science, Latin, and French. He was a member of both the Key Club, which recognized the top 15 percent of the student body in academic achievement, and the Lamp and Laurel, composed of the top twelve students in the school.[15] His grades were good enough for him to graduate in the first quarter of his class and to be accepted at Princeton without having to take the college entrance exams.

At McBurney, Lewis was also a member of the Scroll Club, a service organization that sponsored activities such as spelling bees, hobby talks, vocabulary contests, and debates; and the "M" Club, which recognized students who had earned a letter in a varsity sport. In addition, he served on the student council and was a member of the fencing team, where he was chosen captain during his last year. As a senior, he also served as an associate editor of the school newspaper, the *McBurneian,* overseeing the first issue that fall. By his senior year, he had already planned to become a surgeon, like his father. When the senior class printed their April Fool issue, called the *McBurney Daily Crystal,* which looked ahead to 30 February 1963, Thomas was featured as a celebrated veterinary surgeon who was being sued for ten thousand dollars by a "prominent society matron," who claimed that he killed her pet poodle, Fifi, while under surgery![16] Certainly a gregarious student, he was chosen as the "class gossip" in a poll taken by the senior class. Besides all of his other activities, Thomas also found time for dramatics, playing Bishop Doran in the senior class production of James Montgomery's *Nothing but the Truth* (1916), a situation comedy about a young stockbroker who bets, as a charity stunt, that he can tell the truth for twenty-four hours.[17]

Princeton

Lewis Thomas's father and two uncles had attended Princeton, so the choice was an obvious and perhaps even an inevitable one, although he did apply to Columbia as well. During his freshman year he lived with nine other freshmen in an off-campus rooming house at 15 Dickinson Street because of the shortage of dormitory housing, but by his sophomore year he had moved into the room at 212 Cyler where he remained for his last three years of college. At fifteen, Thomas was young for a college freshman, and the novelty of freedom and lack of parental supervision must have been a heady experience, for as he indicates in *The Youngest Science,* he was a much less diligent student at Princeton than he had been at the McBurney School, turning "into a moult of dullness and laziness" and earning grades of "average or below average in courses requiring real effort."[18] By all accounts, the rooming house on Dickinson Street must have been a chaotic place, with ten lively freshmen rooming together, all on their own for the first time in their lives. Except for a campus proctor, there was no supervision in the rooming houses, and the maids cleaned only once a week. Apparently, no one was particular about housekeeping, and clothes, books, and athletic gear were strewn about until they were ready to be used.[19]

At that time, freshmen at Princeton were required to wear beanies or black caps without visors. Chapel attendance was required of all students on Sunday. Freshmen and sophomores ate in the university commons until their fourth semester, when they were invited to be "looked over" by the eating clubs of their choice. Princeton did not win a major football game during Thomas's years there, so his senior class wore white cotton "beer jackets" with the silhouette of a cow to represent the class motto, "no utter like it," and the inscription "MV-O" ("major victories—none").[20]

In *This Side of Paradise* (1920), F. Scott Fitzgerald portrayed the Princeton undergraduates as a frivolous and irresponsible lot, but the institution was really quite different from that. After Woodrow Wilson became president of the university in 1902, he introduced a series of academic reforms, including a preceptorial system, to change the university from a "place where there are youngsters doing tasks to a place where there are men thinking."[21] He strengthened the requirements in the undergraduate curriculum and fought to reform the eating clubs, which he felt were too restrictive and undemocratic. In place of the "aimless free elective system," Wilson's academic program called for two years of general studies, with a strong classical emphasis, followed by two years of concentrated study in a major field, with electives to be chosen from outside of the major field. All freshmen had to take Latin, English composition, history, and gym, and most elected mathematics and another foreign language. To avoid the problems of the lecture system, students were to meet in small groups with their preceptors and discuss the readings they had prepared beforehand in their courses. Wilson's reforms were intended to promote active learning and critical thinking and to instill his ideal of "Princeton in the Nation's service."[22] Though Lewis Thomas may have been tempted to play Amory Blaine (of Fitzgerald's *This Side of Paradise*) when he came home as a freshman, entertaining his friends with tales of Trenton roadhouses and speakeasies, he was actually embarked on a rigorous course of undergraduate education.[23]

As Thomas indicates in *The Youngest Science*, there was no established premedical curriculum at Princeton during his undergraduate years from 1929 to 1933, so besides majoring in biology and taking the obligatory

physics and two courses in chemistry, he still had room for English or
humanities electives.[24] Apparently he developed an interest in poetry
and read some Ezra Pound and T. S. Eliot during these years, but his
literary interests seemed to be directed primarily toward the *Princeton
Tiger,* the undergraduate humor magazine, for which he wrote light
verse and humorous sketches and on whose editorial board he served.
After his freshman year, he became a member of the Key and Seal
Club, one of Princeton's eating clubs, and otherwise worked only hard
enough to hold his place in "the dead center, the 'gentleman's third'
of the class."[25]

Thomas's literary efforts in the *Princeton Tiger* are interesting if only
to suggest something about his undergraduate tastes and inclinations.
The magazine included cartoons, humorous sketches, and light verse
that parodied or lampooned undergraduate life. Football games, dances,
parties, mixers, weekend drinking escapades, and campus movies were
all duly satirized, as in any collegiate humor magazine. The articles
often strike a tone of bemused tolerance of undergraduate foibles,
perhaps in imitation of the sophisticated style of the *New Yorker,* which
had begun supplying a new model for undergraduate magazines in
1925. The *Tiger*'s format sometimes resembled the smart weekly, but
its contents also foreshadowed the jaded tone of features in *Esquire,*
which Thomas's generation would found in 1933, the year he graduated.
Thomas published several pieces in the *Tiger* during his junior and
senior years, signing his copy "L.T." or "ELTIE." His three poems
that appeared there are witty and clever light verse, in the style of
Ogden Nash, but are otherwise unexceptional. "Reflections on the
Investigation" satirizes the venality of a New York politician; "Reflections
on the Evil of Drink" ridicules those who engage in maudlin introspection
and indiscreet confessions when they've had too much to drink; and
the most interesting, "Disrespectful Note on the Divine Plan," reflects
Thomas's undergraduate religious skepticism.

> By sinning we get lots of things
> To entertain us when we're bored,
> But labored virtue only brings
> Virtue as its own reward.
>
> I think it futile of the Lord,
> To say that goodness should result
> In such a slim reward,
> When goodness is so difficult.
>   L.T.[26]

In much of his juvenilia, Thomas employs a conventional lyric form and shows the fondness for the witty, epigrammatic phrase that also distinguishes his later "good bad verse," as he calls it in *The Youngest Science.*

His humorous prose sketches are more notable for their tone and style than for their substance. Thomas is able to strike a convincing note of jaded, upper-class ennui in viewing freshman behavior at the cinema in "Princeton's Movie Industry"; in the same issue of the *Tiger,* he writes "Something New in Advertising," a clever satire of Madison Avenue advertising copy; "Like a Light" lampoons a weekend drinking escapade; and "The Huddle" mocks a losing football teams's pathetic efforts; but these are largely the clever but superficial efforts of an immature writer trying out the effects of different humorous styles and tones of voice.[27] Some of his other pieces are in notably bad taste, such as his clumsy imitation of a German Gothic murder mystery, "The Horror at Fuhrtbang," and "Christmas Comes to the Jukes Family," a bizarre Christmas Eve story that alludes to the infamous New England family with a history of genetic and psychopathic defects caused by excessive inbreeding.[28] Even as juvenilia, these are clever but uninspired efforts, best forgotten except for what they may have taught Lewis Thomas about where his real talents and abilities lay: not in belles lettres but in science. Otherwise, they confirm that Lew Thomas had a keen sense of humor as an undergraduate. Besides his literary wit, he was known for his off-the-cuff monologues and hilariously accurate impersonations of professors. One monologue in particular, about the function of the frontal lobes, using all of the clichés of polite society, left his listeners weak with laughter.

Fortunately, in his senior year, Thomas took an advanced biology course with a remarkable professor, Wilbur Willis Swingle, which reawakened his interest in science and steered him away from his literary dilettantism. Swingle was an outstanding research biologist who had done important work in the field of endocrinology. He had recently discovered "an extract of the cortical region of the adrenal gland which enabled patients with the deadly Addison's disease not only to stay alive, but to function normally." His colleagues recalled that "for some time his small laboratory in Guyot Hall was the sole source of this extract," and contributions from recipients helped to defray the costs of his research.[29] He carried out many important research projects in endocrine physiology and was the author of more than two hundred papers. A distinguished teacher of both undergraduate and graduate students, Swingle carefully integrated his research efforts with his teaching, directing over thirty doctoral dissertations as well as teaching a famous introduction-to-biology course from 1929 until 1957. No doubt Thomas was inspired by Swingle's teaching and research accomplishments, because by his senior year he had once again become "a reasonably alert scholar." With his interest in academics revived, Thomas applied to Harvard Medical School and was admitted with the help of Dr. Hans Zinsser, a professor of bacteriology. Author of the well-known *Rats, Lice, and History* (1937), as well as the standard textbook in bacteriology, Zinsser had interned with Thomas's father at Roosevelt Hospital and had also known his mother there, so when Thomas met with him during his medical school interview, Zinsser agreed to put in a word for him as a favor to his parents.[30] Apparently Thomas made a good enough impression during his interview to offset his average grades, because after graduating from Princeton with a B.S. in biology in June 1933, he entered Harvard Medical School that fall.

Harvard Medical School

As Thomas indicates in *The Youngest Science,* his medical education at Harvard was not, in principle, very different from what his father received at Columbia College of Physicians and Surgeons a generation earlier.

The details had changed a lot since his time, especially in the fields of medical science relating to disease mechanisms; physiology and biochemistry had become far more complex and also more illuminating; microbiology and immunology had already, by the 1930s, transformed our understanding of the causation of the major infectious diseases. But the *purpose* of the curriculum was, if anything, even more conservative than thirty years earlier. It was to teach the recognition of disease entities, their classification, their signs, symptoms, and laboratory manifestations, and how to make an accurate diagnosis. The treatment of disease was the most minor part of the curriculum, almost left out altogether.[31]

The basic principles, established at the Johns Hopkins Medical School at the turn of the century, called for two years of basic science followed by two of clinical training. These reforms had been set forth in Sir William Osler's *The Principles and Practice of Medicine* (1892) and given additional impetus by the mandate of the Flexner Report of

1910, which to a large degree shaped the course of modern American medical training. As Thomas remarks: "The medicine we were trained to practice was, essentially, Osler's medicine. Our task for the future was to be diagnosis and explanation. Explanation was the real business of medicine. What the ill patient and his family wanted most was to know the name of the illness, and then, if possible, what had caused it, and finally, most important of all, how it was likely to turn out."[32] The assumptions that underlie Osler's medicine were shaped in response to the chaotic, eclectic, and often unprofessional standards of American medical training in the nineteenth century. At that time widespread medical quackery threatened to discredit the profession. A group of young American physicians who had trained in Germany founded the Johns Hopkins Medical School in 1893 with the express purpose of combining thorough training in the basic sciences with a sound clinical education. A standard four-year curriculum was established at Hopkins, beyond the bachelor of arts, consisting of two years of basic science education, followed by two years of clinical training in a hospital setting. Previously, many American doctors were trained using an ineffectual lecture system emphasizing memorization rather than actual patient contact, so that many physicians graduated without ever seeing a patient!

Sir William Osler (1847–1919), in particular, reacted against the absence of rigorous clinical training by introducing "a graded system of postgraduate education for interns and residents which became a model for the postgraduate clinical education in the twentieth century."[33] As his biographer, Harvey Cushing, indicates, "Osler believed in the old maxim that 'the whole art of medicine lies in observation,'" and thus at Hopkins "the student learned the practical art of medicine at the bedside."[34] In addition, "he made students responsible for the history of a patient's illness, for a complete physical examination, and for the simpler laboratory tests."[35] Thus, as Thomas observes, "slowly but surely during the latter part of the nineteenth century, the natural history of disease came to dominate medical education, and the art of making an accurate diagnosis and forecasting the likely outcome of every illness became the highest skill and the indispensable craft of the practicing physician."[36]

The inherent cautiousness of Osler's principles stemmed from his recognition of how little was actually known about the etiology of most disease mechanisms, coupled with the worthlessness of the existing pharmacopoeia and therapeutic practices. Osler emphasized that physicians possess little power to cure and that there are no effective remedies for most diseases, so that instead of expecting to cure patients, doctors should concentrate on accurate diagnosis while pressing forward with medical research wherever possible. He stressed the image of the physician as an educated man, whose professional obligation was to keep up with medical innovations. The profession of medicine, rather than ending with medical school graduation, involved lifelong training. Finally, he emphasized the ideal of medicine as humane service.

The Hopkins model of medical education established a connection between growing scientific knowledge and sound clinical practice, which transformed American medical education and put it on a par with the best German training. It established a pattern of medical education that is still dominant today, though postgraduate medical study has become increasingly important as the pressures to specialize have become more intense. Osler and his colleagues at Hopkins helped to establish the image of the American physician as a scientifically and culturally informed person skilled in diagnosis and prognosis, though his means of therapeutic treatment, once a disease was identified, might be limited. Today, the science of clinical laboratory diagnosis has given the physician powerful new diagnostic tools. Doctors now rely on laboratory tests rather than personal intuition, though the practice of medicine is still empirical in many respects.

Thomas entered Harvard Medical School at a point in the 1930s when medicine began its transformation from a healing art into a clinical science. The doctrine of therapeutic nihilism, which assumed that no treatment is better than an ineffectual or harmful one and that a great many patients have the capacity to get well by themselves, still dominated the profession. While a physician's accurate diagnosis could at least put to rest the patient's anxieties and fears of the unknown, beyond that, little could be done. The medical educators of Osler's generation were determined to abandon the ineffectual or harmful treatments that had been used in the nineteenth century: the cupping, bleeding, blistering, purging, induction of vomiting, and immersion of the body in hot or cold baths, which often did more harm than good. The only really effective medications were quinine for malaria, digitalis for heart failure, and morphine for acute pain.

By the 1930s, a quiet revolution was under way in the clinical laboratories of the Thorndike, Rockefeller University, Johns Hopkins, and a few other research centers. Based on previous discoveries in immunology and microbiology, new pharmaceuticals were gradually being synthesized to combat a variety of ailments: "liver extract for pernicious anemia, insulin for diabetes, the early vitamins, immunization against diphtheria and tetanus, antiserum for pneumococcal pneumonia."[37] Though Thomas and his fellow medical students were taught that the treatment of disease would be the least of their responsibilities, a transformation in therapeutic medicine would soon occur with the introduction of penicillin and the sulfonamides. This change began in the late 1930s, during Thomas's internship at Boston City Hospital, with the successful treatment of pneumococcal and streptococcal septicemia with sulfanilamide.[38] For the first time, physicians had a series of effective treatments for the most common infectious diseases: typhoid fever, lobar pneumonia, tuberculosis, rheumatic fever, and syphilis. Thomas witnessed the introduction of these new antibiotics and was inspired enough by their success to consider a career in medical research.

During his first two years at Harvard, Thomas took the standard medical science courses and a few electives, such as Professor David Rioch's "advanced" neuroanatomy, where he built a plastic model of the brain, and Professor Tracy Mallory's seminar in advanced pathology, but his real clinical education began with the third- and fourth-year clerkships. These clinical clerkships were assigned to students on a competitive basis from among the four teaching hospitals affiliated with Harvard Medical School: Peter Bent Brigham, Beth Israel, Boston City Hospital, and Massachusetts General. Students put in bids for what they wanted, depending on the reputation of the clinical professor and the ward, from among the standard rotations in surgery, pediatrics, obstetrics-gynecology, psychiatry, and internal (or diagnostic) medicine. Harvard was somewhat unusual in that the clinical professors held tenured positions at the hospitals, not the medical school, so after the first two years of basic science courses, the clinical training took place on the wards during the three-month rotating clerkships.

Thomas was fortunate enough during his clerkship to work with some superb diagnosticians among his clinical professors, particularly Dr. Hermann Blumgart, at Beth Israel, who later became a distinguished cardiologist. Blumgart had a knack for quick, intuitive judgment of whether a patient's problem was serious or not and what could be done for the patient. He inspired his students with the thoroughness and care of his physical examinations and with his careful attention to detail in making his diagnosis. A capable medical administrator as well, he fostered the growth of Beth Israel Hospital after its affiliation with Harvard. Blumgart also found time to conduct important research in thyroid and cardiac pathophysiology, collaborating with Dr. Soma Weiss in the first use of radioactive isotopes in human physiology studies.[39] During the 1950s, he edited the prestigious journal *Circulation.*

It was the research opportunities available through the close affiliation with Boston City Hospital and the Thorndike Memorial Laboratories that distinguished Harvard Medical School in the 1930s. The Thorndike was founded by Dr. Francis W. Peabody in 1923 in order to combine the clinical and research study of human disease. Locating a separate research institute adjacent to a major hospital enabled medical students to expand their training in new and promising areas of clinical research. Thomas had the opportunity to study with Dr. George Minot, chief of medicine and head of the Thorndike, as well as 1934 Nobel Prize winner for his discovery of a cure for pernicious anemia; Max Finland, a distinguished immunologist who ran the two infectious-disease labs; and Dr. Houston Merritt, who developed an improved treatment for epilepsy. Infection was the dominant clinical problem then, and members of the Thorndike staff did important work in the clinical evaluation of antipneumococcal sera, penicillin, streptomycin, Chloromycetin, and a host of other new antibiotics.[40] As they witnessed the efficacy of these wonder drugs, the interns realized that these new discoveries were about to change their profession. The days of therapeutic nihilism were coming to an end.

Thomas seemed to enjoy the rigor and intensity of his Harvard years. A bright and capable medical student, full of life and humor, he sometimes wrote light verse or doggerel for the change parties when the clerks rotated or the interns graduated, and he may well have had a hand in the impromptu skits that poked fun at the faculty. During his fourth year, he served on the editorial board of the class yearbook, *Aesculapiad,* and wrote "a long and disrespectful poem about medicine and death," entitled "Allen Street," the common name for the morgue at Massachusetts General Hospital.[41] His academic work was good enough for him to graduate from Harvard Medical School cum laude in 1937.

Internship

Thomas later remembered his internship as one of the most rewarding periods in his life, at least in terms of job fulfillment, though the hours were long and the pay meager. During his final year of medical school he chose to intern at Boston City Hospital, a highly coveted position, where Harvard staffed two of the five clinical services, the second and fourth. Thomas served on the fourth medical division, or Peabody Service, housed in the Peabody Building and named for Dr. Francis W. Peabody, a distinguished practitioner whose *Doctor and Patient* (1930) established high standards of patient care on Harvard's clinical services at Boston City Hospital. During their first week on the wards, new interns were given a copy of Peabody's essay "The Care of the Patient" to guide their clinical training. In this essay, Peabody stressed that while "the treatment of a disease may be entirely impersonal; the care of a patient must be completely personal."[42] Peabody believed that the young physician's success in treating his patients depended on establishing this personal relationship. Thomas was no doubt drawn by the elite reputation of the Peabody Service and by the impressive research facilities offered by affiliation with the Thorndike Memorial Laboratories.

The eighteen-month internship at the Harvard Medical Unit was divided into six periods, or rotations of three months each, forming a clear hierarchy through which each intern moved in progressive steps. The newest intern, or junior, also known as the "pup," did all the scut work of collecting patient specimens and doing the necessary diagnostic laboratory work for his ward of thirty patients.[43] Dr. Eugene Stead, who was a clinical resident at the Thorndike Memorial Laboratory ward during Thomas's internship at Boston City Hospital, remembers him as a diligent and efficient intern who did his work well. His patients' X rays and lab tests were always there when the house officer requested them, but most important, he seemed to be enjoying his clinical training. He was the kind of intern who made the daily rounds pass more quickly because of his cheerful and cooperative attitude. Dr. Stead recalls that even among a highly competent group of interns, Thomas stood out as a promising clinician.[44]

As Thomas mentions in *The Youngest Science,* the medical students and interns learned as much from each other as from their clinical professors, and shaped each other's careers in ways unrecognized at the time.[45] Perhaps the most influential role model and mentor for Thomas, in terms of his later career as an essayist, was Franz Ingelfinger, another young intern, about a year ahead of Thomas in rotation, with whom he developed a friendship. Ingelfinger, who later became a distinguished gastroenterologist and editor of the *New England Journal of Medicine* from 1967 to 1980, was, in Thomas's words, "a born teacher." Not only did he teach Thomas the necessary clinical skills, such as improvising a makeshift oxygen tent, pumping the stomach of a comatose patient, or finding a vein for an injection, but after hours they would listen to recordings of Mozart in Ingelfinger's apartment, while he pointed out distinctive phrasings in a particular movement.[46]

Ingelfinger was a brilliant only child in a distinguished German-American family, his father a physician and professor of bacteriology at Gottingen, and his mother an energetic New England teacher. Their son Franz Joseph was born in Dresden, but the family later fled Germany after World War I and settled in New England. He attended Andover and Yale, where he majored in English and took a broad variety of liberal arts courses besides playing football. He decided on medical school because of the lack of job prospects during the depression years and was admitted to the Harvard Medical School class of 1936.[47] Since he was Thomas's senior in rotation, Thomas got used to taking orders from him, a relationship that, as Thomas humorously admits, later led to his automatic acceptance of Ingelfinger's offer to write a guest column for the *New England Journal of Medicine* in 1971. On Christmas Eve in 1937, when Thomas was on duty on the wards, he tacked the following note on Ingelfinger's door:

> Of Christmas joy I am the bringer,
> I bring good news to Ingelfinger.
> Though many turned in bed and cried,
> Nobody died, nobody died.[48]

On the hospital wards, however, Thomas's droll wit and irrepressible humor were sometimes misunderstood by the other interns. "Once when a particularly obnoxious and obese patient entered with a stroke," Ingelfinger later recalled, "Lew at that time a senior himself, told his pup to give the patient a huge and toxic dose of morphine with the expectation, of course, that the new intern would recognize the absurdity of the dose and the total lack of seriousness of Lew's suggestions."[49] Thomas was horrified when the dose was actually given to the patient, but fortunately it was not lethal and the patient recovered. Later Thomas would write that the best four years of his life included his time as house officer on the Peabody wards (1937–39) and the period he spent in clinical research at the Thorndike (1941–42).

It seems to me now, almost four decades later, that I've been coasting along ever since on what I learned in that short span of time. I learned all I know about looking after patients from Castle, Minot, Keefer, Weiss, Finland, Williams, Stead, Meiklejohn, Stevens, Strauss, Place, and most especially the Peabody nurses whose names, I regret to say, I've forgotten. I learned how to set up laboratory experiments at first hand from John Dingle and Max Finland, and I've not forgotten a moment of it. The richest of all experiences was being junior house officer to Franz Ingelfinger, who taught me, among many other things, how to listen to Mozart and how to worry endlessly about patients.[50]

A Poet on the Wards

Salaries at Boston City Hospital were so low during the 1930s that interns had to depend on blood donations, at twenty-five dollars a pint, for extra cash. At some point during Thomas's internship, he accidentally found a way to use his literary talents to supplement his meager income. While he was on the fourth service, as he recalls, he often had insomnia and so he wrote verse late at night, while on call, on the typewriter in the secretary's office on the top floor of the Peabody. One night he accidentally left a folder of his poems behind and they were discovered by Dr. A. P. Meiklejohn, a Scottish physician working on vitamin B research at the Thorndike. Meiklejohn liked the poems so well that he sent copies of them to Russell and Volkening, a New York literary agency. Thomas was not informed of this, so he was surprised to receive a letter from the agency several weeks later, offering to place the poems in magazines. Eventually he published about a dozen poems in the *Atlantic Monthly, Harper's Bazaar,* and the *Saturday Evening Post.*[51]

While none of these poems shows exceptional ability, they are more thoughtful and mature than his Princeton juvenilia and show some modest literary ambitions. Perhaps Thomas's most gratifying response, besides the publisher's checks, was the note he received from Dr. George R. Minot, chief of the Harvard Medical Services, congratulating him on his literary efforts, after his first poem was published in the *Atlantic.*[52]

The poems Thomas published in the *Atlantic* in 1941 show a new maturity and awareness brought on by wartime conditions and by his medical experience. In "Vitamins—1941," one finds an ironic contrast between the role of vitamins A through E in enhancing human life and the destructiveness of mass warfare.[53] In each stanza of this prose poem, Thomas names the beneficial qualities of a vitamin and then adds a parenthetical refrain describing a destructive act of war. The poem implies that the horrors of modern, mechanized warfare have undercut any advances medical science has made to improve human health.

Many of these poems are simple four-stanza lyrics in iambic tetrameter, using an *a b a b* rhyme scheme or ballad form. The unusual subject matter often contrasts strongly with the conventional lyric form. "Millennium," for instance, imagines the moment of death in naturalistic terms as a soft hush, a snuffing out of the senses, particularly the sounds of war, which are replaced by the rustling of leaves and a quiet breeze.[54] What is interesting here is the ironic note in the last stanza, suggesting a time in which the earth sighs in relief, finally to be rid of man. "Design for Heaven, 1941" continues this same disparaging treatment of conventional Christian notions of the afterlife. Here heaven is conceived as a suburb enjoying eternal spring, with the "Souls of the Departed" rocking on the porches of their endlessly similar homes. This apparent bliss is undercut by the surrealistic image of the Deity as a "shining clock" with no hands, hanging in place of the sun.[55]

Several other poems are more closely related to Thomas's medical experiences. "Ward One" describes the wards of alcoholics and derelicts in Boston City Hospital, strapped to their beds during their periods of delirium.[56] "Tombstone Inscription," perhaps based on Thomas's experiences during the hectic period of the influenza outbreak of 1940–41, employs a terse style reminiscent of Emily Dickinson, with spare syntax and an ironic personification of Death as "nervous," "fallible," and "careless," moving warily, as if stalking his prey.[57] One should never predict the end of life, the poem cautions, because Death is slow and "weary," and "never done," for it must subdue "each reluctant cell," as the body struggles to live, and breath remains on the mirror.

Residency and Marriage

Thomas had always been interested in neurology and at one time had even wanted to become a neurosurgeon, so halfway through his internship in 1938, when he learned that Dr. Robert F. Loeb would become the new director of the Neurological Institute of New York, at Columbia Presbyterian Medical Center, he decided to apply for a residency there. He was accepted and began his residency in 1939. Soon afterward, a new director, Dr. Tracy Jackson Putnam, arrived from Harvard to reorganize the research program by creating a laboratory to study brain abscesses in experimental animals in order to devise better treatments for humans. Thomas was able to begin his research work in Dr. Putnam's laboratory in the summer of 1940, and he published his first scientific paper soon thereafter.[58] He was particularly interested in the baffling disease of multiple sclerosis and offered a hypothesis that it might result from an autoimmune reaction directed at the patient's own brain tissue.[59] After completing his residency in 1941, he was appointed the first Tilney Fellow in Neurology at the institute. With the assurance of an $1800-a-year income and the prospects of becoming chief resident there, after another year of study at Harvard, he decided to get married.

Thomas had met his future wife, Beryl Dawson, at an undergraduate mixer while he was at Princeton and she was attending Vassar. Later she dropped out of Vassar to study in France. Perhaps because she lived abroad with her diplomat father, Vassar did not hold her interest. She lived in Kew Gardens in Queens, not far from Flushing, so it was not difficult for them to see each other whenever Thomas was home on vacation. They were a well-matched couple, with her vivid personality and good taste balanced by his wit and perspicuity. On the morning of 1 January 1941, they were married in the chapel of Grace Church in Manhattan and left for Boston that afternoon.[60]

Chapter Two
A Medical Researcher

No sooner had Lew and Beryl Thomas settled into their new apartment on Longwood Avenue in Boston than a call came to move John Dingle's laboratory at the Thorndike up to Halifax, Nova Scotia, to help authorities contain an outbreak of bacterial meningitis at a Canadian military installation there. Because of wartime conditions, the Nova Scotian health authorities did not have adequate staffing to deal with the epidemic, so they requested help from Harvard.[1] When the Thorndike team arrived, Thomas was put to work screening patients, collecting fluid specimens, and treating confirmed cases with the new antibiotic sulfadiazine. The staff then recorded the clinical course of the disease under treatment and collected additional cultures to bring back to Boston for further study. The Thomases spent about a month in Halifax, with Beryl recruited as a laboratory assistant to keep records and help with the shipment of the cultures.[2] The new sulfadiazine treatment for meningitis was so successful that Thomas and Dingle announced their results in a clinical paper published in 1943.[3]

After they returned to Boston that spring, Thomas continued his study as a research fellow and assistant in medicine at the Thorndike Memorial Laboratories. He was particularly interested in understanding the effects of the meningococcus bacterium on the brain and spinal cord. In the course of his work, he discovered that conventional laboratory animals—rats, rabbits, guinea pigs, and mice—have a natural immunity to the meningococci. But, paradoxically, this natural immunity could be destroyed by injecting the rabbits with suspensions of heat-killed meningitis cultures.[4] Since this phenomenon was not understood, Thomas hoped to conduct further studies of this primitive "prozone" reaction, in which a laboratory animal could lose its natural immunity as a result of being inoculated with excessive antigens of a particular bacterium. However, World War II intervened, and he never got a chance to answer this question or to return to the Neurological Institute. Though he did not return to neurology after the war was over, Thomas still regards it as "the most fascinating of all fields of medicine" because of the multitude of unanswered questions regarding the biochemical functions of the brain and the mechanisms of many serious diseases of the brain.[5]

The Rockefeller Institute and Naval Research

As the United States mobilized for war in the Pacific, immediate research was needed to cope with the threat of tropical diseases that might affect Allied landing forces on Japanese-held islands. Military planners turned for help to the major civilian medical research centers. "The Rockefeller Institute in New York was put on notice in late 1941," as Thomas recalls, and "then mobilized as a naval medical research unit."[6] Thomas was commissioned as a lieutenant junior grade in the U.S. Naval Reserve and assigned to the Rockefeller Institute as a visiting investigator. His orders were to report for duty by the end of March 1942, so the Thomases packed up to return to New York, along with their daughter Abigail, who had been born in Boston on 13 October 1941.

At the Rockefeller, Thomas went to work for Dr. Thomas M. Rivers, a well-known virologist who was later to become Thomas's predecessor on the New York City Board of Health. Lew was given four research assignments, the most important of which was to study scrub typhus, or tsutsugamushi fever, a highly lethal disease known to exist on Japanese-held islands in the Pacific. His other lab assignments were to isolate a virus from military patients with primary atypical (or viral) pneumonia and to study the disease vectors of psittacosis, or "parrot fever," both of which were highly contagious diseases. His safest task was to run pregnancy tests on urine specimens from Navy Waves.[7] He spent the summer of 1942 as a visiting investigator in Norman Topping's laboratory at the National Institutes of Health in Washington, D.C., continuing his work on scrub typhus. Throughout that year, he worked in labs containing highly lethal organisms, often without adequate safety precautions and at considerable risk to his health. One of the senior staff in Topping's lab later died of scrub typhus contracted from airborne rickettsias from a Waring blender that had been opened prematurely.[8]

The Rockefeller Naval Research Unit no. 1 was assigned to the Pacific campaign in 1943, and preparations began to mobilize the unit. Extra staff had to be hired and the necessary equipment purchased to assemble a set of portable research units that could be rapidly reconstructed wherever they were needed. These preparations in New York took over a year, and the unit was not ready to leave for the West Coast until the fall of 1944. During that same year, Thomas's second daughter, Judith, was born on 6 March.

The personnel and equipment for Research Unit no. 1 traveled by train to California, where the staff were assigned to basic training at the San Bruno Military Base, near San Francisco. Their unit, composed of biological and medical specialists, must have seemed like unpromising academic types to the marine officers assigned to train them. During their basic training maneuvers on the cliffs overlooking the Pacific, they were taught how to handle the Browning automatic rifle. One of their colleagues, a nearsighted entomologist, was sometimes distracted by insect specimens in the grass. Once he absentmindedly swung his loaded automatic rifle around and pointed it at the drill sergeant and class, who hurriedly took cover and yelled at their colleague to aim his gun back over the ocean before he fired it.

Guam and Okinawa

The Rockefeller unit somehow survived basic training and shipped out to Honolulu, where they joined up with a convoy headed for Guam. There they reassembled their portable labs without the help of the Seabees and set to work on their investigations. They discounted the risk of scrub fever on Iwo Jima after they discovered that the necessary vector, a particular species of mite, was not present. Then they were assigned to study the causes of an outbreak of infectious hepatitis in the Philippines, and smaller teams were detailed to accompany the planned Okinawa invasion.

Thomas left Guam with Richard Shope's team in late March 1945, aboard an army transport vessel bound for Okinawa. They arrived offshore from Naha on 3 April, two days after the invasion had begun, while the battle for control of the island was still under way. The transports and supply vessels sitting at anchor were the targets of waves of Japanese kamikaze raids. When Thomas's medical research unit was finally sent ashore, he climbed down the ropes and waded to the beach carrying a cage full of white laboratory mice, much to the amusement of the battle-hardened marines, who commented that now they had seen everything! Thomas found no scrub typhus on Okinawa, though they were faced with an outbreak of a malignant form of encephalitis, capable of being transmitted to American troops via mosquitoes. The medical researchers were finally able to leave Okinawa in September, though their plane lost an engine en route to Guam and was forced to return for repairs. Thomas spent the remainder of his active duty in Guam studying the pathology of rheumatic fever, using experiments involving laboratory rabbits. He was successful in inducing cardiac lesions by using injections of heat-killed streptococci and homogenized rabbit heart tissue, but unfortunately he neglected to bring the original laboratory animals back with him and his results could not be replicated back in the States. Thomas was discharged as a navy lieutenant commander in the Medical Corps and returned to the Rockefeller Institute in New York, and to his wife and children, by January 1946.

Pediatrics and Poetry at Johns Hopkins

Thomas was fortunate enough to be part of the post–World War II period of expansion and growth in American medical research, when opportunities were abundant and frequent career moves not uncommon. Within a decade, Lew and Beryl Thomas moved fifteen times, living in New York, Baltimore, New Orleans, and Minneapolis. Their first relocation after the war was to Baltimore, in 1946, where Thomas accepted a position as an assistant professor of pediatrics at the Johns Hopkins Medical School and as a pediatrician at the Harriet Lane Home for Invalid Children, Johns Hopkins Hospital. While they were in Baltimore, their third daughter, Eliza, was born on 4 April 1948.

Along with Thomas's clinical and teaching responsibilities at Hopkins, he also had an opportunity to conduct research on rheumatic fever in children. Thomas suspected that rheumatic fever was another case of an excessive immunologic reaction by the body's own defense mechanisms. The disease begins as a localized streptococcus infection, but after this initial stage has passed, there is the danger of permanent heart-valve damage as an aftereffect of the original strep infection. Thomas discovered that initial treatment with cortisone actually helped to spread the infection by suppressing the body's ability to fight off the streptococcus bacteria. His research into the pathology of rheumatic fever led to his theory that "much, if not most of the damage caused by disease results not from anything intrinsically toxic about the invader but from a misreading of signals by the host, which then unleashes an overwhelming and inappropriate defense reaction; these defense mechanisms may cause the damage."[9] This important insight into the role of the immune response in the etiology of disease has informed much of Thomas's subsequent medical research. It is also the subject of his longest and most technical essay in *The Medusa and the Snail,* appropriately entitled "On Disease."

After arriving in Baltimore, the Thomases settled into a comfortable flat in a brownstone on Park Street, across town from the Hopkins medical laboratories. The upstairs tenant was a Hopkins speech and drama professor, Elliott Coleman, who was also a poet. Thomas and Coleman shared an interest in writing poetry and encouraged each other's work. In the evenings, Coleman would drop in on the Thomases and read from his verse or discuss Thomas's medical research. This encouragement stimulated Thomas's interest in poetry and got him writing again.

During the war years after 1941, Thomas published only one poem, in the *Atlantic,* "Limitation," which expresses something of his personal philosophy in terms reminiscent of Alexander Pope's "Essay on Man." Despite man's ability to measure and quantify his world, the poem implies, he cannot escape the limitations of his nature.

> Paint the moon and hoist the planet
> Ride as fast as ever can.
> Still, in any ticking minute,
> Man is limited to man.[10]

Consistent with his medical humanism, Thomas implicitly denies any supernatural dimension to human existence. Instead, he believes that man is capable of solving his problems using the resources of his mind. Apparently Thomas found this kind of guarded optimism congenial to his scientific temperament, for the dual themes of human limitations and hope frequently appear in his verse.

In 1948, Thomas published an interesting set of three poems in the short-lived *Hopkins Review,* based in part on his clinical experience at Hopkins.[11] These poems show an advance in metrical technique beyond the simple tetrameter stanza of his early work, as well as a willingness to experiment with a narrative, free-verse form in at least one poem, "Meditation—103 Fahrenheit." The first poem, "Ward Rounds," describes the toxic-induced delirium of gravely ill patients who mutter in their sleep or call out meaningless phrases as death approaches. Stanzas 1 and 2 contrast the speaker's empathy and compassion for the patients with the cold indifference of the clinical professor, who diagnoses the illness and instructs his interns on "the business of death." In the last stanza, the unconscious patient is oblivious to the ward rounds and to the approaching footsteps of Death, who whispers to the students, "it is near. / How are you now involved? What do you fear?"

The second poem, "Meditation—103 Fahrenheit," describes the onset of a strep infection from the point of view of both host and invader, patient and bacterial cell, as the speaker, "sick with chills and the fever," convalesces while the infection is slowly destroyed. The progress of the disease is described in terms of the conventional metaphors of invasion and battle, although who is the host and who the parasite is deliberately left ambiguous. Turning tables, the poem asks ironically, "For whom then is who then infective?" recognizing that the body's defenses against the strep infection will ultimately prove more lethal for the (perhaps unwilling) invader than for the host. As he hopes for a truce, the speaker wonders whether the fate of the strep bacteria is not more bitter than that of the only temporarily ill patient.

The last poem in the series, "Plant a Metal Seed," questions the value of human technological prowess that enables us to tell time by latitude anywhere on the globe, send our words out into space, or program our thoughts on metal cards, but leaves us naked and vulnerably human beneath our technological armor. No fruit will ever mature, the poem warns, from the "artificial flower" born of "a metal seed in concrete bed." Thomas's perspective here becomes more emphatically humane and man-centered, in the Oslerian tradition, despite his deep involvement with the new medical technology and research that were beginning to transform American medicine during the late 1940s. Unfortunately, these were the last poems Thomas would publish for more than two decades, until "On Insects" appeared in the *New Yorker* in 1971.[12] The demands of medical research and administration, as well as his growing family responsibilities, did not allow him the leisure or reflection necessary to compose verse, and what free time he had Thomas preferred to spend in the laboratory, where he could immerse himself in some interesting new research problem, a form of recreation he preferred to a game of bridge or other more conventional forms of entertainment. Even after he became a full-time medical administrator, Thomas always liked to have access to his own personal laboratory as a place to unwind from the pressures and responsibilities of his position.

New Orleans and Minneapolis

After two years at Hopkins, Thomas was feeling restless in pediatrics and was eager to return to internal medicine or neurology, so when he was offered a position at Tulane University directing their new research program in microbiology and immunology, he readily accepted. Moving was difficult with two young children and a new-born infant, but the Thomases arrived in New Orleans by June, to face the sweltering humidity of unair-conditioned housing in the Garden District. Because of the postwar housing shortage, they found temporary quarters in a large house that had been subdivided into apartments, later moving into renovated army barracks on the Tulane campus. Thomas immediately started work at Charity Hospital, where his responsibilities included managing the infectious-disease clinic, and proceeded to set up his research laboratory at the medical school.

By his second year at Tulane, Thomas had assembled a small but talented group of investigators to study the pathogenesis of experimental allergic encephalomyelitis (EAE), a neurological disease in dogs with some striking similarities to multiple sclerosis (MS) in humans. Dr. Philip Y. Paterson, a young research colleague at Tulane, remembers Thomas as a vibrant and energetic researcher with the scientific curiosity and imagination to follow up obscure leads and unlikely connections in the course of his research. Part of Thomas's creativity came from his willingness to risk unorthodox approaches and his "refusal to adhere to prevailing dogma in vogue concerning whatever research issue he is concerned with at any point in time."[13] Thomas worked with extraordinary intensity in the lab, intuitively grasping the significance of work in progress and throwing out new ideas in a rush of words and phrases when he really became excited about a research lead. Then he would stand beside the lab bench, "blue eyes flashing, tremulous fingers pointing, every muscle tensed to contain his burning excitement." In the evenings he would sometimes return to the lab after midnight to redesign an inconclusive lab procedure. Even during his vacations, he could not put aside his lab research. When Thomas and his family went north for an extended summer vacation on Long Island, New York, in 1949, he fired off daily letters to his lab associates with questions, suggestions, and requests for progress reports. Often his suggestions were remarkably farsighted and prescient, as when he suggested in an August 1949 letter to Dr. Paterson that he "look for brain antigen in the cerebrospinal fluid (CSF) of MS patients," an idea about fifteen years ahead of its time. Paterson cites this example to demonstrate how Thomas's refusal to be dogmatic or to accept the prevailing view of a research problem often led to original and unexpected hypotheses. It was later discovered, as Thomas had suspected, that "the

MS-susceptible individual would appear to have lost normal immunologic tolerance of his own neural self-antigens, thereby unwittingly mounting an immune attack against his own CNS (Central Nervous System) as if he is trying to reject it, not unlike the rejection of a renal allograft (kidney transplant)."[14] Thomas had a gift for inspiring young medical students and postdoctoral research fellows with the creative excitement of medical research, and many of his former students, like Dr. Paterson, have made important contributions in areas of medical research, such as in understanding the role of neuroimmunologic mechanisms in the pathology of multiple sclerosis.

Thomas and his family had scarcely settled into New Orleans when, two years later, in 1950, Dr. Irvine McQuarrie offered him a chair in pediatrics and medicine at the University of Minnesota Medical School and the newly constructed Variety Club Heart Hospital in Minneapolis.[15] When Thomas and his wife went up to Minneapolis to consider the offer, he was so impressed with the new research facilities there that they decided to make the move back north, where they found the cooler climate exhilarating and the intellectual and cultural climate more hospitable than in New Orleans. The Thomases promptly bought their first house, a white frame bungalow in St. Anthony Park, and put down roots there for five years. It was the first time that Thomas had to shovel snow since leaving Flushing.

In Minneapolis, Thomas was responsible for organizing a research unit for both the pediatrics and medicine departments at the new hospital, and he quickly attracted a talented and enthusiastic group of young bacteriologists and immunologists to his lab. In 1951, he organized an important symposium on rheumatic fever, attracting the major researchers on the pathogenesis of inflammatory and immunologic diseases.[16] Shortly afterward, he was named American Legion Memorial Heart Professor, and the pathogenesis of rheumatic fever remained the focus of his research during his Minnesota years.

According to Dr. Lewis W. Wannamaker, a member of Thomas's research team, "Thomas was intrigued by the notion that rheumatic fever might result from a continuing, occult infection with group A streptococci." Thomas and a fellow researcher, Dr. Floyd Denny, showed that these bacteria "could persist in the heart and organs of rabbits for long periods of time after experimental infection and that cortisone would induce streptococcal bacteremia in some of these rabbits."[17] Their work led to Thomas's publication of a caution against the use of cortisone in treating the primary strep infection in humans because of the danger of suppressing the body's natural immune defenses against secondary infection.

Rheumatic fever, a complex and baffling disease of childhood and early adulthood, was an especially serious problem on American military bases during World War II. As a result, several epidemiological studies were commissioned to investigate its causes and prevention. It was established that the disease was caused by secondary complications of a group A streptococcal infection, or a strep throat. These secondary effects, which often appear after the initial infection, can be quite severe and may include damage to the heart muscle or valve tissue, enlarged heart, congestive heart failure, endocarditis, arthritis, or chorea. The pathogenesis of rheumatic fever fascinated Thomas, as he remarked in an article in *Minnesota Medicine*.

A constant stimulus to research on rheumatic fever is [its] very complexity. It is difficult to study any disease for any length of time without becoming possessed by the feeling that it contains universals: that if we had the answers to the questions it raises we would understand a great deal about disease in general. Another human ailment has been called the "great imitator." Rheumatic fever might well be called the "great original." All parts of the body participate . . . and it involves the blood vessels and connective tissues everywhere. It has for some students the appearance of an infection, to others it seems the result of an infection, and to others a misguided defense against an infection. Its conceivable implications for other human diseases extend in all directions, encompassing conditions as unrelated as disseminated lupus erythematosus, Rocky Mountain spotted fever, malignant hypertension, eclampsia, and glomerulonephritis. It constitutes a working model for the study of all diseases of the vascular tree, perhaps including even the changes which occur in aging.[18]

In 1948, a group of medical researchers led by Dr. Charles Rammelkamp at the Warren Air Force Base in Cheyenne, Wyoming, discovered that the risks of rheumatic fever could be greatly reduced by antibiotic treatment with penicillin during the initial stages of the strep throat infection, a discovery for which they later won the Lasker Award.[19] Dr. Floyd Denny, one of the members of Rammelkamp's research team, later came to work with Thomas in Minnesota in the fall of 1951, and they began trying to create an experimental model for rheumatic fever.

As an experimental pathologist, Thomas was intrigued by any animal model that offered a close approximation of a human disease mechanism, and for a while he thought that the Shwartzman reaction in rabbits might offer some clues to the development of rheumatic fever in humans. If a rabbit is given an intravenous dose of a bacterial endotoxin and a second dose eighteen hours later, the second dose will cause lesions throughout the body similar to rheumatic heart lesions. The parallels were clear enough that for a time, Thomas and Denny thought they might be close to a breakthrough in understanding the pathogenesis of rheumatic fever. This was not the case, however, since their results could not be replicated, and unfortunately the biomechanisms of this disease are still not fully understood. But for Thomas, the study of rheumatic fever raised some fundamental issues about the nature of disease. Why do some streptococcal bacteria cause rheumatic fever, while others do not? Why are some patients so much more susceptible than others? Why are the effects of the disease so varied, so that one patient suffers damage to heart muscle leading to permanent heart disability, while another patient suffers from chorea? And why the often delayed or regressive appearance of the disease? Thomas's medical curiosity was piqued by these unexplained phenomena for what they might reveal about the mechanisms of infectious and degenerative diseases.

Nor was Thomas's curiosity limited to the rheumatic fever problem. He was particularly intrigued by experiments that led to droll or unexpected results. For instance, he discovered that a reversible collapse of rabbits' ears could be induced by intravenous injection of crude papain, which temporarily dissolves the cartilage matrix of the ears, causing them to droop. The limp rabbit ears would gradually recover their strength after a few days, except when cortisone is administered. Thomas did not discover the explanation for this curious phenomenon until some years later, during a sabbatical at Cambridge, England, when he found the same disintegration occurring with embryonic mouse bones in a colleague's research.[20]

As one of his Minnesota colleagues recalls, the Thomas lab was always an interesting place to work. Thomas might design an animal experiment with one hundred rabbits divided into ten experimental groups, each intended to investigate a different question, but he rarely maintained controls because he was too impatient to learn the results and often would not bother to replicate his experiments himself, leaving that to others. As the experiment progressed, Thomas would sometimes sacrifice the experimental animals prematurely and at random from each experimental group instead of waiting until the end of the trial run or until they died of the disease effects. He had a quick, incisive mind, and once he learned what he wanted, he would drop a problem or leave it with others to complete. His mixing of the control animals sometimes frustrated his fellow researchers, as would his tendency to carry his lab results in his head instead of entering them in lab notebooks, but this approach was due more to his driving curiosity and his desire to know than to any disdain for normal lab procedures. Thomas also believed that a bench scientist should always have more than one experiment going at the same time, so that in case the results of the primary experiment proved disappointing, there would always be a "potboiler" in progress with predictable results to sustain lab morale.

On a typical day, Thomas would come into the Minnesota lab at about nine, have a brief meeting with his colleagues to review any new results or findings, and then carefully monitor the design groups before settling down to his own bench work. Though he would leave by five or six to be with his family, he often returned to the lab later in the evening. He suffered from intense insomnia and kept a lab notebook by his bedside in which to jot down ideas, or else he would come back to the lab late at night to redesign an experiment or modify some work in progress. His fertile mind was a constant source of new ideas, even though he may not always have possessed the patience or concentration to see his work to completion. But he was generous in sharing his ideas with his colleagues, many of whom later built their own careers developing ideas suggested to them during their work with Thomas. He had a unique gift for creating the kind of encouraging and supportive atmosphere in which good research flourishes, a visionary imagination that asks the right experimental questions, and the ability to inspire and assist others with their own research and to communicate his sense of the excitement and fun of science. A particularly striking new lab finding, such as the appearance of fibrinoid (a tissue or muscle disintegration occurring as the result of an immune or inflammatory reaction) in a tissue sample, would excite him so much that his hands would become white and cold from a circulatory problem he had. As he peered into a microscope, he would jokingly ask a colleague to feel his hands whenever he came across an impressive result. These same qualities of intellectual excitement, driving curiosity, and enthusiasm for pure research science became apparent later in his essays when he began to write for the *New England Journal of Medicine*.

The NYU Years

In the spring of 1954, Thomas gave a talk on the Shwartzman reaction before the Streptococcal Commission of the Armed Forces

Epidemiological Board, emphasizing the importance of endotoxin as the central focus of all biological transactions. His remarks so impressed the audience that Dr. Colin MacLeod of New York University Medical School invited Thomas to come to New York to head the pathology department there. The former chairman of pathology had just retired, and Thomas's charge was to rebuild a program that had been depleted by retirements and resignations.[21] Thomas also hoped to reorient the department away from the traditional field of hospital pathology and into the new field of experimental pathology in order to recruit young scientists who could work in close conjunction with the departments of immunology and microbiology to investigate the immunologic aspects of human disease mechanisms. He wanted to move NYU's pathology program in the direction of the broader and more innovative English university model, with its emphasis on the study of disease mechanisms, rather than the traditional American model, which was oriented more toward anatomy. The NYU Medical School had earned an excellent reputation through its work in the area of infectious disease immunology during the 1940s and had excellent faculty in other clinical sciences as well. As Thomas recalls: "I was attracted by the world's finest microbiology department. The presence of people like MacLeod, Pappenheimer, and Bernheimer—as well as Ochoa in biochemistry and Bernard Davis in pharmacology—made the offer of a job at NYU irresistible."[22]

Thomas was also instrumental in transforming immunology from its infectious-disease origin, in which the basic research was done by microbiologists (or bacteriologists), into a new clinical science with its focus on the study of the immune system, with investigations centering on immunochemistry and cellular immunology. During World War II, NYU researchers had done important work in the study of infectious-disease mechanisms, but by the late 1940s, "there was a growing perception that immune processes might be involved in other types of human disorders."[23] As Thomas recalls: "It had been suspected for some time that rheumatic fever was in some sense an abnormal immunological reaction (to streptoccocal infection) and rheumatoid arthritis was under suspicion as based on a similar mechanism. The whole notion of autoimmune mechanisms in the causation of disease was becoming a very lively notion in medicine and pathology. It began to look to a good many people as though research in immunology might uncover some important mechanisms that did not seem approachable by other scientific avenues."[24] By expanding the scope of experimental pathology, Thomas succeeded in gathering together a "critical mass" of talented investigators in immunology; he encouraged their research endeavors during the seminal years, gathered funds, laboratory space, and support from the medical school, and solicited funds from the National Institutes of Health. In short, he presided over the emergence of the new field of cellular immunology during its "golden years" in the 1950s.[25] As Thomas recalls: "Actually, it turns out, not being a genuine pathologist was something of an advantage. I had a rather free hand to recruit a number of people who later turned out to be important—and whose scientific commitment was in the field of immunology."[26]

The word soon got out about Thomas's new appointment, and he received inquiries from a number of promising young researchers who hoped to work with him at NYU. Thomas was a keen judge of character and intellect and did not hesitate to reach abroad to Europe to find talented and creative minds. During his tenure in pathology at NYU, he built an international research team that included Baruj Benacerraf, Zoltan Ovary, Jeanette Thorbecke, Al Stetson, H. Sherwood Lawrence, Howard Green, and many others. As one of Thomas's colleagues recalls, his approach to recruitment was quite original. "He would go off to Europe, bump into one or two interesting, unusual scientists along the way who were investigating an area which, at that point, might not be particularly popular. He'd have one or two conversations with them, and the next thing, a couple of strange people would appear in the hallway. They'd bring unusual techniques, problems, and perspectives. We became a very heterogeneous department, filled with scientists doing their own, interesting things."[27]

The researchers that Thomas recruited were attracted by the excellent reputation of the NYU program. The basic research for at least one Nobel Prize in medicine was done at NYU during Thomas's years as chairman in the 1950s: Baruj Benacerraf's pioneering experiments delineating the genetic control of the immune response. Many of the medical students and research fellows who trained at NYU later went on to initiate medical research programs at other major universities, so that NYU Medical School became second only to Harvard in training its graduates to enter the field of academic medicine, a record in which Thomas took great pride. During his fifteen years at NYU, Thomas also initiated the Honors Program at the Medical School, and helped to design the first combined M.D.-Ph.D. program in the country, which subsequently became a model for others of its kind. He established pathology seminars and an Immunology Club where faculty could discuss their current research findings with their colleagues. His goal was to create an open and supportive climate for innovative research where medical researchers could share their findings and learn from each other. Thomas envisioned an educational climate at NYU that encouraged excellence in both basic science and clinical work, where medical students could integrate their studies so as to excel in both areas. He believed in breaking down institutional and departmental barriers in order to create a research faculty "without walls." As a result of Thomas's recruiting, the pathology labs became crowded with researchers, who were forced to share equipment and work in cramped, noisy, but intellectually lively quarters. As Thomas recalls, the crowding may not have been a bad thing, because people were forced to collaborate, and sharing equipment often led to sharing ideas as well. His colleague and 1980 Nobel Prize winner Baruj Benacerraf agrees. "In a crowded laboratory you must keep your wits about you—keep on your toes. Tight circumstances stimulate creativity. Whenever you see a laboratory that is not crowded, you know it's dead."[28]

Nor did Thomas's own research suffer during these years from 1954 to 1958, when he chaired the NYU pathology department. About this time he first proposed his immunological surveillance theory of cancer, which was later expanded on by Sir MacFarlane Burnet.[29] Basically, Thomas theorized that there may be a single triggering mechanism for a variety of different cancers, all caused by a mysterious failure of the body's immune system to recognize and eliminate carcinogenic cells before they metastasized. Thomas's theory has not been widely accepted, but as H. Sherwood Lawrence has noted, his insights have been tragically vindicated in the etiology of AIDS, or acquired immunodeficiency syndrome, in which a viral-induced suppression of the normal activity of the human immune system leads to a whole host of secondary complications, including the rapidly progressive Kaposi's sarcoma; rectal, gastric, and skin cancers; non-Hodgkin's and Burkitt's lymphoma; as well as a variety of infectious disorders that are ordinarily controlled by the T-helper cells.[30] Later, in 1963, Thomas helped to organize the International Symposium on Injury, Inflammation, and Immunity, sponsored by Miles Laboratories, which brought together leading clinical and research investigators to review the latest findings concerning the immunologic response to physical and chemical injuries, the clinical aspects of immune-type reactions, and the immune mechanisms that lead to tissue injury. He was one of the editors of the proceedings from the symposium and contributed an article on the action of cortisone in reactions to tissue injury.[31]

By 1958, the immunology program was well underway at NYU, and Thomas was ready for new challenges. He had always admired Bellevue as the model of an excellent urban teaching hospital, and a commitment to universal quality medical care, regardless of the patient's ability to pay, had been instilled in him during his internship with the Harvard Medical Service at Boston City Hospital, so when the opportunity arose in 1958 for him to chair the Department of Medicine at Bellevue, he quickly accepted the appointment. In fact, when Thomas first came to interview at NYU in 1954, a colleague took him over to Bellevue Hospital to visit one of the senior pathologists, who was recuperating as a patient there after an illness. Thomas was so stimulated by the hospital surroundings that he spent just a few minutes with the patient and then requested a tour of the hospital! From 1958 to 1966, during his period at New York University–Bellevue Medical Center, Thomas served as director of the third and fourth medical divisions of Bellevue Hospital, president of the Medical Board at Bellevue, and director of medicine at University Hospital. During the summer months of 1959 and 1960, Thomas took a temporary sabbatical from NYU and Bellevue to conduct research on the human placenta at Cambridge University in England. But his primary concern remained his administrative responsibilities at Bellevue and NYU.

The oldest public teaching hospital in the nation, Bellevue traces its origins back to an almshouse founded in 1736 on the present site of city hall. Originally a workhouse and infirmary for the city's poor, the almshouse was moved to a site called Belle Vue Farm during the yellow fever epidemic of 1794, and its name was officially changed to Bellevue Hospital in 1816.[32] For 140 years, the NYU School of Medicine has enjoyed a special relationship with Bellevue as its principal teaching hospital, and the Bellevue Hospital Medical College formally merged with NYU in 1898. Until 1968, Bellevue and NYU maintained an informal understanding that NYU medical faculty would attend at Bellevue as voluntary physicians. In that year, when Columbia and Cornell withdrew their medical services, NYU was left with the sole responsibility for medical staffing at Bellevue, and the relationship between the hospital and the university was formalized. The NYU medical faculty have shown a unique degree of loyalty and humane commitment to providing quality medical care for the indigent of New York, and in return, Bellevue has offered the medical school an incomparably varied setting for clinical training. Though the NYU School of Medicine is also responsible for staffing the Manhattan Veteran's Administration Hospital and the private University Hospital, Bellevue remains at the core of NYU's teaching program. As Thomas commented during the 1960s, when he was dean of the School of Medicine: "For all its faults, and they are numberless, we do not believe there is a better place to teach medicine on earth. Even with a new University Hospital and a large VA Hospital on our campus, which could provide more teaching beds than most medical schools possess, and in the face of pressure to shift our teaching programs before the roofs of [old] Bellevue literally cave in on us, our faculty and students still prefer to remain based in Bellevue."[33]

By the 1950s, the old Bellevue Hospital was a dilapidated structure, with long open wards, filled, as Thomas recalls, with the sickest and poorest patients; as a public hospital, Bellevue was obliged to treat them all. After World War II, a $50 million bond issue was passed by the city of New York to build a new Bellevue Hospital facility, but the money was diverted to construct the Bronx Municipal Hospital instead. For the next twenty years, the hospital was inadequately funded by the city until a group of three university medical-service heads, including Thomas, formed the Better Bellevue Association to lobby the city for a new structure. In 1957, Dr. Dickinson Richards of Columbia, a Nobel Prize winner, charged that Bellevue's facilities had deteriorated to a dangerous level, but changes were slow to come, given the climate of New York City politics.

One of Thomas's major contributions during his time as chairman of the Department of Medicine was to persuade the city of New York to build a new Bellevue Hospital. This involved taking on the city administration and the entrenched bureaucracy, but Thomas proved as persistent in political lobbying as he had been in supporting medical research at NYU. Along with Dr. Richards of Columbia and Dr. Thomas Almy of Cornell, Thomas spent countless hours at city hall trying to get sufficient money allocated to relieve the chronic shortages of supplies and to repair the decrepit facilities at the old hospital until the new building could be completed. The budgetary problems were created by the centralized administration at New York City's Department of Hospitals and by the Department of Purchase and the Bureau of the Budget, which often failed to spend the money appropriated for the hospital. Thomas's answer was to create a "quasi-public corporation, patterned after the Port Authority of New York and New Jersey," to wrench the budgetary control away from city hall, but the result was only to create another layer of bureaucracy.[34]

The ground breaking for the new Bellevue Hospital took place in 1961, but it took fourteen years and numberless delays before the new facility was fully completed and operative in 1975. For several years, in fact, construction moved no further than a large excavation hole, nicknamed the "Bellevue swimming pool," which sat and collected water, as Thomas describes in his essay "Ponds." While the new facility was under construction, Thomas was making his clinical rounds with a younger colleague and he stopped to examine a patient while the pile drivers outside were making it all but impossible to hear anything above the noise of the construction. The old Bellevue Hospital had two wings, A and B, next to which the new building was being erected. Thomas looked up from his patient and remarked, as he removed his stethoscope: "One thing is sure. Wing A is louder than Wing B!" These were difficult times for Bellevue, which saw other municipal hospitals expanding and modernizing with the aid of federal funds. Medicare and Medicaid patients chose newer, more comfortable hospitals nearer to their homes, and Bellevue's patient load declined so drastically that its future as a teaching hospital was thrown into doubt.[35] But since the new facility opened in 1975, this trend has reversed and Bellevue is again attracting new patients with its improved facilities and excellent tertiary-care programs, especially in the areas of emergency medicine, cardiology, and geriatrics. Of the quality of medical care at Bellevue, Thomas has commented, with obvious loyalty: "I regard it still, as I did when I walked through the unhinged doors of the old building, as the most distinguished hospital in the country, with the most devoted professional staff. If I were to be taken sick in a taxicab with something serious, or struck down on a New York street, I would want to be taken there."[36]

Another important public service Thomas performed was in agreeing to serve on the New York City Board of Health, to which he was nominated in 1956 to succeed his old boss, Dr. Thomas Rivers of the Rockefeller Institute, who had just retired. During his fifteen years on the Board of Health, Thomas dealt with such controversial issues as the dating of milk and the fluoridation of the New York City water supply, and he pressed for action in new areas of concern, such as heroin addiction, neighborhood health clinics, and poor housing. To alleviate the city's growing heroin problem, he proposed the idea of free, drop-in neighborhood health clinics that would dispense a controlled supply of methadone to heroin addicts. The neighborhood health-clinic concept was never funded because of New York City's fiscal crisis, but

Thomas published his proposal in an essay entitled "Heroin" in the *New England Journal of Medicine,* though he later omitted it from *The Lives of a Cell.*[37] Perhaps Thomas's most successful administrative innovation, however, was the establishment of the Health Research Council, which helped to fund research in areas of pressing health concerns and provided fellowship support for young medical researchers who wanted to work at medical schools in the New York metropolitan area. As the heroin-addiction problem became increasingly serious during the 1960s, Thomas persuaded a young colleague, Dr. Eric Simon, to take on the question of the biochemistry of opiate addiction, with the resulting discovery that the brain manufactures its own painkilling substance, endorphin. Another colleague of Thomas's, Dr. Vincent Dole of the Rockefeller Institute, suggested that methadone might be used as a substitute for heroin in helping addicts to break their habit, an idea that Thomas promoted at the Board of Health. The Health Research Council program was initially funded at a figure of a dollar per citizen, and it was later estimated that it generated a tenfold return in jobs and resources for the original investment.[38] Working on the New York City Board of Health also helped to arouse Thomas's concern for social justice, a concern he later brought to the deanship of the NYU School of Medicine during his appointment from 1966 to 1969.

By 1966, after Thomas had served for eight years as chairman of medicine at Bellevue, he was offered the deanship of the New York University School of Medicine. He served there for three years during a period of expansion, and later at Yale during a period of retrenchment in federal funds for medical research. Thomas sought to broaden the admissions policies at NYU, already a relatively liberal institution, helping more native New Yorkers, women, and minority students gain access to medical school. These policy changes reaffirmed the university's mission, as expressed in its motto, "a private university in the public service." In his dean's note in the NYU Medical School yearbook from 1967, Thomas appealed to the social conscience of his students, as future physicians, reminding them that the "hardest, most nearly insoluble problems for the physician" are in the cities, yet the opportunities for service there, in hospitals such as Bellevue, are also considerable, and he praised the energy of the young as a major resource in solving social problems.[39] Skeptical of the trend toward increasing medical specialization, he believed that medical students should balance their clinical training with medical research experience. Once when someone asked him where to go for postdoctoral training, he replied facetiously:

"Obviously you should work with the best person you can find, but as an M.D. you should go into a nonclinical department, and as a Ph.D. you should work in a clinical department. That way you can't be imposed upon and your time is your own." Once, when he came across one of his research fellows in a Bellevue ward studying for his boards in internal medicine, Thomas quipped: "Why bother? I've never taken Boards in any of these areas."[40] His own training had been in academic medicine, and with his commitment to medical research, he had no need to be certified in clinical medicine.

Thomas's own style as a clinician was to be more theory- than problem-oriented. The theory of disease and disease processes fascinated him, and his patient rounds at Bellevue would become ad hoc clinical conferences for his students. He was a shrewd diagnostician who could ask penetrating questions and quickly elicit the clinical information he needed. With his intellectual excitement he could take even a mundane subject and make it interesting. He approached clinical problems as biological puzzles to be solved and during clinical rounds often discussed how diseases were generated. Both the patient and the disease process were of keen interest to him. What one learned from Thomas was a certain attitude toward medicine as an endlessly fascinating area for investigative research. He was equally open and flexible in dealing with alternative theories of disease and with more mundane matters of curriculum or rules. His restless and inquiring mind was matched by the brisk pace of his clinical rounds, which often forced students or colleagues to hold impromptu conferences with him while he was en route to one meeting or another.

Thomas believed that medical students should be broadly educated in the humanities as well as in clinical training in order to make them better physicians, so along with a colleague, Dr. Zoltan Ovary, he helped to initiate a medical humanities program at NYU, bringing in outside musicians such as Albert Fuller, a faculty member at the Juilliard School, who organized a chamber music concert series at the medical school from 1961 to 1972. As "musician-in-residence" at the NYU School of Medicine in 1967–68, Fuller arranged a Renaissance and baroque concert series, with musicians using the original instruments and arrangements whenever possible. Thomas enjoyed listening to classical music because he felt that it externalized the human thought processes, and in several of his essays he has written of his love for the music of Johann Sebastian Bach and Gustav Mahler. In the summer of 1982, he even agreed to lecture on the philosophy of science and art at Fuller's

Aston Magna Academy in the Berkshires but was forced to withdraw because of health problems.[41]

Even with his busy administrative schedule, Thomas never lost his clinical concern for others. He once left his office and drove to a colleague's Park Avenue apartment, after a frantic call from the man's wife, to help reinsert her father's catheter tube, which had fallen out. In another incident while he was dean, Thomas sent an administrative assistant back to his (Thomas's) apartment with a grandchild's baby shoe that the toddler had put in his briefcase. When Thomas pulled the shoe out of his briefcase, he remarked absentmindedly: "Oh, there it is. We've been looking everywhere for it!"[42] At NYU, Thomas was noted for his laissez-faire style of administration—he believed in a minimal amount of interference as long as things were operating smoothly. The dean's job is to ensure financial stability and to facilitate the work of the faculty. Otherwise, according to Thomas, a healthy university regulates itself, rather like a large organism. He also had a superb instinct for knowing when he had accomplished all that he could at a particular administrative assignment and when it was time to bow out. Perhaps it was this instinct that led to his surprising decision to accept an appointment as chairman of the Department of Pathology at the Yale–New Haven Medical Center in 1969, or perhaps he simply missed his lab research. At Yale, he assumed the Anthony N. Brady Professorship in Pathology, which did not carry any clinical responsibilities and left him largely free to pursue his interests in the pathogenesis of mycoplasma diseases.

Yale Medical School and Sloan-Kettering

Thomas had long been interested in the related diseases of the autoimmune system, and his move back to experimental pathology at Yale gave him the opportunity to return to his research into the causes of rheumatoid arthritis, a baffling and crippling degenerative disease that attacks the tissues and joints. Although the exact causes of this disease are still unknown, the standard theory is that it may be the result of an autoimmune disorder, in which antibodies are formed against one's own joints. Thomas's own theory, however, is that rheumatoid arthritis may be the result of an infection caused by mycoplasmas, an anomalous class of bacteria that somehow exist without cell walls. No one has succeeded in cultivating these strange pathogens from joint fluid or tissues of patients suffering from the disease, and little is known about how they survive or cause disease in their hosts. Thomas devoted much of his research time at Yale to the study of mycoplasmas and their possible link to rheumatoid arthritis, and to the related problem of inflammation.[43]

In his lab on Cedar Street, he ran a number of simultaneous ongoing animal studies involving mycoplasma infections with promising analogues to human illnesses. His lab assistant, Dorothy McGregor, was kept busy ordering turkeys, guinea pigs, hamsters, and rabbits for these often unpredictable studies. He never used controls in his initial experiments and usually kept the results in his head. He liked to guard his privacy and would not keep regular office hours, even after he became dean of the Yale University School of Medicine in 1972, a position he did not actively seek. Thomas kept his paperwork to a minimum and did his own typing and scheduling of appointments, which kept his secretary eternally confused. He worked at a large, open table in whose single drawer he filed unimportant memos, on the theory that if a problem was important, he would hear about it again. His office adjoined the lab, allowing him a convenient exit to his lab to avoid being bothered by inopportune visitors. Often he would finish his paperwork behind closed doors, to the accompaniment of Bach's "Brandenburg Concertos," which he had taped as background music. He once told a research colleague: "I will appear to be inaccessible, but I'm really not. Just knock on the door if you need me."[44] But Thomas's style was to suggest a promising research problem and then leave his lab associates free to pursue their work in their own way. Occasionally he would check by to see if any interesting results had turned up, but otherwise he ran a small, rather informal lab with one lab assistant and a technician. His research style was more intuitive than systematic, and he was brilliant at intuiting results even from inconclusive data.

One problem that particularly fascinated him was why penicillin was lethal to guinea pigs, except during certain seasons. He theorized that the intestinal flora in the animal might be susceptible to the antibiotic, and that the guinea pigs then died of secondary complications. Thomas was also interested in why penicillin is effective against infectious bacteria, and he suggested that it might interfere with the synthesis of bacterial cell walls, creating altered, L-forms of the bacteria that are more susceptible to the body's immune defenses. One of his research colleagues was working with Syrian hamsters in an attempt to find an experimental model for mycoplasmal pneumonia. He was getting mixed results, and after scanning the data, Thomas remarked: "The hamster is a very private person. They either look fine or they're dead. They hide inside all that loose skin and show no appearance of illness."[45]

Thomas also maintained his privacy and his mobility during his Yale years. In 1971, he was invited to visit as guest lecturer at the University of California Veterinary School at Davis, where he was impressed with the quality of the students, whom he compared favorably with the medical students he had taught. During this time, he also became increasingly involved in foundation and scientific advisory work, where his opinions and expertise were often called upon. He served as a member of the NIH National Health Advisory Council, the Public Health Research Institute, the President's Science Advisory Council, the President's Biomedical Research Panel, and the National Advisory Council on Aging, as well as numerous private philanthropic and science foundations, university boards of trustees, and honorary organizations. In this capacity he was a vigorous advocate of funding for pure rather than applied medical research. In testimony before the Senate Committee on Appropriations in February 1972, Thomas remarked:

If I were a policy maker, interested in saving money for health care over the long haul, I would regard it as an act of high prudence to give high priority to a lot more basic research in biologic science. This is the only way to get the full mileage that biology owes to the science of medicine. . . . I do not believe in the biological inevitability of disease. I see no reason to suppose that heart disease is a natural part of the human condition, and I am convinced that cancer will eventually be entirely curable. I believe that we should be able to rid ourselves of the disabling diseases associated with aging, particularly stroke. My point is that when we are successful in these ventures, the cost of health care will tend to go down rather than up.[46]

Perhaps his favorite research institute was the Marine Biological Laboratory in Woods Hole on Cape Cod, which Thomas enjoyed visiting on summer weekends when he drove up from New Haven to listen to the Friday evening lecture and meet with friends and associates to share the latest scientific findings. During this time, the Thomases bought a house on Cape Cod so that he could pursue his new interest in symbiotic relationships among marine organisms.

In May of 1972, Thomas was named the eleventh dean of the Yale School of Medicine, a position he held for less than a year before resigning in February 1973. Given Thomas's interest in promoting medical research, perhaps it is not surprising that when he was offered the presidency of the Memorial Sloan-Kettering Cancer Center in 1973, he quickly accepted. Originally founded in 1884 as the New York Cancer Hospital, with a dual emphasis on the study and treatment of cancer, the institution experienced several name changes before becoming affiliated with the Sloan-Kettering Institute in 1960. Thanks to the generous philanthrophic support of a number of benefactors, the combined hospital and research center erected new facilities on the upper East Side of Manhattan, adjacent to Rockefeller University and New York Hospital–Cornell Medical Center. As the new president and chief executive officer, Thomas presided over the opening of the new 565-bed Memorial Hospital in November 1973.[47] Through his leadership, the center assumed a prominent role in international cancer research, treatment, and education, becoming one of the three comprehensive cancer centers designated by the National Cancer Act. In 1980, Thomas was appointed the first chancellor of Memorial Sloan-Kettering, and he served in this role until he became chancellor emeritus in 1983. The pressure of administrative responsibilities and his new writing career forced Thomas to shut down his personal lab during this decade, but he continued to closely follow the research of his colleagues, particularly the work being done with olfaction, tracking, and genetic self-recognition by Drs. Edward and Jeanette Boyse. Thomas was intrigued that congeneric strains of laboratory mice could be trained to distinguish their own genetic lines from others strictly by smell, a discovery that he felt might have immunologic implications for the acceptance or rejection of tissue or organ transplants.[48] Thomas proposed that "histocompatibility genes might impart to each individual a characteristic scent," which could be identified by dogs specially trained to distinguish among human tissue types.[49] If the biochemistry that determines our individual uniqueness has an olfactory expression, then it is even conceivable that humans could learn to distinguish among the HLA (human leukocyte antigen) types of other individuals.[50]

In this research and in other areas as well, Lewis Thomas has shown remarkable prescience both in his sense of the implications of his own and his colleagues' medical research and in his ability to foresee what would be important in the future. His ability to grasp the biological essence of new areas of research has enabled him to direct and support the investigations of his junior colleagues and fellows in the most productive areas. One of his NYU colleagues called him "a uniquely gifted scientist with a broad overview of what medicine is about."[51]

Throughout his career, Thomas has been convinced that the only real advances in health come from a basic understanding of disease processes and the application of that knowledge to public health. Recognizing that modern medicine has increasingly become biomedicine, he has been a firm supporter of basic biomedical research. His commitment to experimental pathology led to later research achievements in such areas as the "biological properties of endotoxin, the pathogenesis of the Shwartzman reaction, the *in vivo* action of papain on cartilage, the action of vitamin A and cortisone on lysosomes, and various immunologic, pathologic, and toxicologic aspects of mycoplasma infection in experimental animals."[52] Though in recent years Thomas has been primarily involved with medical administration at Sloan-Kettering, he has continued his investigations of the genetic significance of self-marking oderants in mice and the capacity of trained dogs to distinguish among HLA types in humans.

In his tribute to Thomas on the occasion of a symposium held in his honor at the NYU Medical Center on 22 November 1982, Dr. Saul Farber commented:

> As the father of modern immunology and experimental pathology, your interests and research have dwelt on the disordered functions caused by the imbalance created by infecting organisms and the defenses of our bodies. Classic and noteworthy among your many innovative and imaginative research contributions have been the studies of endotoxin, the toxic substance retained within the body of harmful bacteria, and on a ubiquitous and pervasive agent of inflammation which is the smallest known free-living organism, the mycoplasma. From these elegant studies you formulated the lucid and visionary concept of immunological surveillance of cancer—a shift in the biological checks and balances resulting in the proliferation of wild neoplastic cells. The cause of and cure for cancer has been brought closer to reality by researchers who follow this lead.
>
> Your concepts of biological systems of life make us aware of the essentiality of organization, communication, and interdependence among simple and complex organisms. The lowly ant and the destructive termite have been raised to lofty heights by your wonderment, expressed in poetic descriptions of their dependence on an organized society with lines of communication that are mysterious to us. In your imaginative perception, these creatures follow natural laws of symbiosis applicable to man and his environment.
>
> Nature is your fascination. With insight, clarity, wit, and poetry, you have educated, stimulated and entertained many, many thousands throughout the world. Your essays, orations, and prize winning books have transformed darkness into light, pessimism into optimism, and ignorance into understanding and knowledge.[53]

During the 1970s, Thomas's fascination with nature found a new form of expression as he turned from medical research to the personal essay and reached out to a new audience, through his columns in the *New England Journal of Medicine* and *Discover* magazine, and through his award-winning books, returning to belles lettres through the encouragement of his old friend and mentor, Franz Ingelfinger.

Chapter Three
The Physician as Essayist

In 1970, while Thomas was chairman of the Department of Pathology at Yale Medical School, he was invited to give the keynote address at a June symposium on inflammation, sponsored by the Upjohn Company in Kalamazoo, Michigan. His assignment was to say something informal but provocative, to offset the heavy tone of the more technical papers and to give some focus to the conference by deliberately presenting a somewhat unorthodox view.[1] His address, "Adaptive Aspects of Inflammation," was recorded along with the conference proceedings, and several months later Thomas received a copy of his talk, which had been reproduced and sent to the conference participants. A few days later, as Thomas recalls in *The Youngest Science,* he received a telephone call from his old friend and former mentor at Boston City Hospital, Dr. Franz Ingelfinger, now editor of the *New England Journal of Medicine.* Ingelfinger had read Thomas's article and liked it so much that he proposed that Thomas write a monthly essay for the *Journal* in the same style and manner. Thomas demurred at first, but the terms were so attractive that he finally agreed to Ingelfinger's proposal. Basically, Thomas was free to write on any topic of his choice, as long as his essays fit the column format of the *Journal's* editorial page (about one thousand words). A new essay was due on the third Thursday of each month. Thomas would not be paid for his work, but there would be no editorial tampering with his essays either.

The concise, lucid style of Thomas's essays was at least partially the result of this unusual editorial agreement. Ingelfinger's offer of editorial freedom combined with a strict length limitation attracted Thomas because it allowed him to compress his thoughts and to express complex ideas as simply as possible. He was tired of the drab style of scientific papers and was eager to try his hand at the informal essay. At first he tried to limit his focus to specific medical topics, but he soon found that he preferred to address a wide variety of scientific and nonscientific issues through the medium of the personal essay. Writing his monthly column, "Notes of a Biology Watcher," enabled him to develop his skills as an essayist before a select and highly intelligent audience, and so he began a productive relationship with the *Journal* that lasted for almost ten years, until Ingelfinger's death in 1980.

After about six months, Thomas felt that he had written enough and wanted to stop, but Ingelfinger was so impressed with the readers' response, including a call from Dr. Francis Cabot Lowell, a prominent Boston physician and classmate of Ingelfinger's, that he urged Thomas to continue. A year or two after his essays began to appear, Thomas received a congratulatory note from Joyce Carol Oates, praising his essays and urging him to consider collecting them in book form. Thomas had also received several editorial inquiries from publishing firms in 1973, but he could not spare the time from his dean's responsibilities at Yale Medical School to complete the kinds of transitions and rewriting they requested, so the projected book remained unfinished until Elisabeth Sifton from Viking Press offered to published the twenty-nine essays as they were, without extensive revision, and *The Lives of a Cell* appeared in 1974.[2]

The Lives of a Cell

The twenty-nine essays collected in *The Lives of a Cell* represent a selection of those Thomas published in the *New England Journal of Medicine* between May 1971 and February 1974.[3] Thomas arranged the collected essays in their order of publication, with the exception of "The World's Biggest Membrane," which he used as his concluding selection. He omitted one essay, "Heroin," perhaps because it did not fit the overall theme of the collection. Because the collected essays appear almost exactly as they were initially published in the *Journal*, *The Lives of a Cell* was a relatively easy book for Thomas and his Viking editors to assemble, but it also gives his readers the opportunity to follow Thomas's development as an essayist from 1971 to 1974. Thomas seemed to find a congenial essay style and voice fairly quickly, and once he established it, he did not deviate much in subsequent essays, at least during the nine years that he wrote for the *Journal*. Altogether, Thomas published fifty-two essays in the *Journal*, and all but three later appeared in his three essay collections.[4] His columns appeared less frequently after 1974 and were published irregularly once Thomas took on his new responsibilities as chancellor of the Sloan-Kettering Cancer Center in New York.

In these essays, Thomas employs a distinctive style noted for its brevity and informality, its crisp factuality, dry humor, and cheerfully optimistic outlook. He often adopts the tone of an old-fashioned family physician dispensing no-nonsense advice to his patients, though he can be whimsical or philosophical as well. His credentials as a physician, cancer researcher, and medical administrator lend unquestioned authority to his essays, but it is his style and vision that have won him such high praise in reviews by Joyce Carol Oates, John Updike, and others.

With more than two hundred professional articles to his credit, Thomas is no stranger to scientific discourse, but the informal essay demands a different voice, more general and less impersonal than the technical article. The great temptation for most scientists is to hide behind the passive voice. This may serve to emphasize the content of professional articles, but it misses the mark in the familiar essay. Essays require a light, deft touch, combined with a quiet and unobtrusive voice that wins the respect of the reader without either insisting too strongly on its own importance or being lost in the impersonality of the passive voice. Any hint of egotism or self-importance will immediately put the reader off as a breach of literary etiquette, while the official scientific style dulls the reader with its pretense of objectivity. Thus the writer of the familiar essay walks a fine line between revealing too much or too little about himself.

The author's persona must be appealing enough to make us want to read and learn more about him. The first-person point of view, by projecting the author's personality through his views and opinions, enlivens and invigorates the author's material, framing it within his unique consciousness. That impulse to share the idiosyncrasies of one's personal tastes, interests, and outlook has always made the personal essay one of the most charming and intimate of literary forms, the one that comes closest to sharing the pleasures of good conversation with an interesting friend. This is precisely the kind of informal, intimate voice and style that Thomas manages to convey in his essays.

The typical Thomas essay employs a plain style with few adjectives or modifiers and relatively simple syntax, often using coordinate construction. Many of his essays are written in the first person. Often he will open with a rhetorical assertion, which he expands with a series of intriguing examples, illustrations, anecdotes, or speculations. As he develops a topic, he combines expository, persuasive, and reflective modes, using examples drawn from medicine or biology as a springboard for more daring philosophical reflections. The Thomas voice is curious, cultured, erudite, and humane, reflecting the Anglo-American medical tradition, established by Sir Thomas Osler, that the physician be more than a narrow specialist. The variety of Thomas's essay topics suggests the breadth of his interests, ranging from Iks (an African tribe) to computers, pheromones to biomythology, insect behavior to etymology— all interesting and provocative topics, discussed in a manner at once witty, sensible, and disarmingly profound.

In *The Lives of a Cell,* Thomas moves easily from micro- to macrobiology, guided by his insatiable curiosity about the natural world. The journals listed in his reference notes—*Science, Scientific American, Nature*—give some indication of the breadth of Thomas's interests in collecting information for his essays. His instinct for what is important allows him to assimilate new scientific ideas and present them in clear and understandable form. The range of his background reading recalls Merlyn's advice to the young Arthur in *The Once and Future King* that the best remedy for sadness is to learn something new.

Despite the diversity of Thomas's interests, a number of common themes appear throughout his essays. Contrary to the prevailing cultural pessimism about the misuse of science, Thomas remains optimistic about the prospects for medical research and for modern science in general. We are a young species, he insists, still profoundly ignorant about ourselves and about the world around us. He reminds us that we are essentially social animals, hopelessly addicted to communication and biologically programmed to create language. His holistic philosophy envisions the earth's biosphere as one vast, interconnected organism somehow groping toward consciousness, with "the beginnings of a nervous system and fair-sized ganglions in the form of cities."[5] In such a world, cooperation counts for more than brute competition and the highest form of cooperative learning is perhaps reflected in the collective enterprise called science. Man's purpose is to exercise his curiosity, to learn, and to exchange information—it's programmed into our genes. Given this benign optimism, Thomas has some reassuring things to say about the human condition, though he is certainly aware of the risks of unrestrained militarism and the threat of nuclear war.

Altruism, cooperation, and symbiosis are the dominant themes in *The Lives of a Cell,* and Thomas's essays are unified by his global, ecological perspective. The behavior of social insects fascinates him, and he draws some interesting sociobiological analogies in comparing ant colonies and termite mounds with out modern cities. Our present codes of social and political behavior, based on outmoded assumptions of innate human aggressiveness and competitiveness, are inadequate, Thomas asserts, since most living organisms cooperate rather than compete and even disease is more often the result of misread biochemical signals than of a wholesale invasion of the host by "hostile" microorganisms. Thomas implies that we are limited in our understanding of the natural world by the inappropriate metaphors that we employ to facilitate our understanding of natural processes. Indeed, competitive Darwinian metaphors are notably absent from Thomas's view of nature, in which he finds most living forms tending toward balance and harmony within their immediate environment rather than dominance and control. Natural ecosystems are characterized by balance and stability, or stasis and equilibrium, buffered against the fluctuations of the external environment, especially in the supply of nutrients and other essential needs.

In fact, Thomas goes so far as to question the whole concept of separate biological identity. Close examination reveals that each level of organization, from ecosystem to atom, is constructed of equally complex subunits—a sort of infinite regress. Far from simple, our cells incorporate smaller, complex microorganisms as permanent endosymbionts. "It might turn out," Thomas speculates, "that the same tendency underlies the joining of organisms into communities, communities into ecosystems, and ecosystems into the biosphere."[6] In fact, the closer we look at the ways in which living organisms function, the more we find ecological communities rather than independent species. Nor of course does man exist apart from the rest of life, for even as he radically transforms the terrestrial environment for his own uses, he still finds himself inextricably embedded in nature.

Cooperation involves communication, which Thomas finds at all levels of life, from the simplest biochemical exchange of molecules between cells to the rich, abstract complexity of human language. From the twitching of termite antennae to the most advanced science lecture, social organisms show a compulsion to communicate, and Thomas is intrigued by the possibility of a built-in, genetic basis for language as a distinctive human trait, like nest-building or hive-making, that sets us apart from the rest of life. Encoded in our DNA may be the ability to generate grammar and syntax in meaningful patterns or even, for some of us, to combine musical notes and harmonies into the most exquisite melodies. If language, art, and music are at the core of our social existence, as genetically determined mechanisms, then there must be some hope for our species after all. Thomas's deep interest in the biological roots of human expression mark him as a most original scientific mind, one willing to risk unorthodox speculations and intuitive leaps into new and uncharted areas of human thought.

Sources and Background. Many of Lewis Thomas's students and colleagues have commented on his talents as a biological theorist, his ability to generate unique and original hypotheses from his experiments. He is especially good at reflecting on the implications of science, in perceiving the unforeseen connections and wider implications of his own and others' work. Nowhere is this gift more apparent than in the remarkable essay entitled "Adaptive Aspects of Inflammation," which Thomas delivered at the Upjohn symposium on inflammation in 1970.[7] Not only does this essay draw some fascinating evolutionary connections between inflammation and symbiosis, but it also serves as a valuable thematic introduction to his first two essay collections, *The Lives of a Cell* and *The Medusa and the Snail*.

Thomas opens his discussion by denying that inflammation exists as a discrete biological phenomenon—rather it is a series of "independent and separate mechanisms"—but he then proceeds to consider it as a single mechanism for the sake of argument. He raises the question of why organisms produce inflammation in response to an incursion by a foreign organism, when the reaction is often more harmful to the host than to the invader. Like hunting waterfowl with tactical weapons, the inflammatory reaction of dog skin to a tick bite or the disabling lesions of rheumatoid arthritis are responses in which the body's defense mechanisms seem "mistaken, inappropriate, and unquestionably self-destructive."[8] When the body's defenses overreact in this way, the result resembles disease, but Thomas speculates that the inflammation reaction may have evolutionary significance as an expression of individuality, "as a defense of an individual against all the rest of nature, symbolizing his individuality and announcing his existence as an entity."[9] According to Thomas, inflammation may well represent "a great natural force for the preservation of species, for protection against all kinds of foreignness."[10] It may be nature's way of distinguishing between self and nonself.

Thomas was clearly fascinated with Lynn Margulis's *Origin of Eukaryotic Cells* (1970), in which she hypothesized that all multicellular life on earth originated from symbiotic, or mutually beneficial, relationships among primitive prokaryotic (prenuclear) cells during the Precambrian era.[11] Margulis speculated that different parts of the eukaryotic (truly nucleated) cell originally may have been free-living prokaryotic organisms that were endosymbiotically incorporated into other prokaryotic cells. The fact that mitochondria and chloroplasts have different DNA and RNA than their hosts lends credence to this hypothesis. Since the prokaryotic cells were the first living organisms to appear on earth, some form of cellular evolution had to proceed before more complex organisms could emerge.

Margulis's theories inspired Thomas to think about the question of differences between cell, organ, organism, and ecosystem. Although his essays are not at all derivative, Thomas was clearly inspired by Margulis's work in his own efforts to articulate a biological definition of individual identity and to establish the connections between cellular evolution and immunology. He realized that both these fields relate to the question of biological identity and that in nature distinctions between species are not always as clear as we might think. Thomas also realized that given the incredibly intricate organization of the eukaryotic cell, its evolutionary history must have implications for the study of the immune reaction and other defense mechanisms.

Borrowing from Lynn Margulis's thesis about the evolution of eukaryotic cells from symbiotic relationships among prokaryotes, Thomas suggests that there is a universal tendency for living forms "to join up, to undergo fusion, to reunite, that the mechanisms we call defensive are designed to counter," so that the opposite of symbiosis is inflammation.[12] Perhaps the inflammation reaction is a kind of "failed symbiosis"? Or could it be a result of the tension between being an individual and being a complex? Thomas then discusses Margulis's hypothesis about symbiosis on the cellular level—the incorporation of blue-green algae into plant cells as chloroplasts and of bacteria into all cells as mitochondria—and points out how the close symbiotic relationships between the free-living precursors of these organelles and their hosts allowed them to be permanently incorporated into the host cells. Thomas finds something inherently "good-natured" about all symbiotic relations and suggests that the amiable relations between organelles and their host cells may offer a new "natural law" to take the place of social Darwinism.

According to Thomas, it is difficult in many symbiotic relationships to tell who is host and who is symbiont, as in the case of the nitrogen-fixing bacteria that live in the root nodules of leguminous plants, without whose presence the plants could not survive. When symbiosis is not mutually beneficial, we call it predation or parasitism, although—as in inflammation—the problem may lie in the inappropriate response of the host, and not in the virulent effects of the parasite. Cell fusion represents another instance in which the boundaries between individual organisms become blurred as membranes join and cells exchange cytoplasm, finally becoming a single hybrid cell. In "Some Biomythology," Thomas even humorously finds examples of symbiosis in the medieval bestiaries, with elaborate composite beasts, such as the griffon, centaur, manticore, and phoenix, serving as mythical archetypes of symbiosis in nature. "There is a tendency for living things to join up," he observes, "establish linkages, live inside each other, return to earlier arrangements, get along, whenever possible. This is the way of the world."[13]

Thomas's interest in symbiosis clearly predates *The Lives of a Cell*. In an earlier article, "Sensuous Symbionts of the Sea," he commented that "the tendency to live together in close partnerships may represent the most ancient habit of all living things."[14] Symbiosis is most prevalent in the sea, where life began, and many marine relationships are extraordinarily specific. Damsel fish live unmolested among the tentacles of sea anemones; algae have adapted to life on the exposed siphonal tissues of giant clams; barnacles fasten themselves to whales; other anemones live on the shells of crabs; and of course there are the medusa and the snail. "Nothing lives alone," Thomas remarks. "One cannot find a genuinely solitary form, uncoupled from everything else. Instead, life is a dense, shimmering matrix of live tissue, in which the creatures of the sea spring to view as working parts, like cells in tissue or organs in an organism."[15]

What are the biochemical determinants, Thomas wonders, that permit these creatures to seek each other out? Perhaps the protein markers of individuality are the forerunners of immunologic mechanisms, except that they serve to bring creatures together rather than keep them apart. Yet another example of symbiosis is incorporation, in which separate individuals come together to form a cluster, or superorganism, during one part of their life cycle. One-celled slime molds coalesce to form a solid multicellular organism with a fruiting stalk to propel spores; marine algae form thick, stratified mats along the shoreline; the sea sponge can be broken down and reformed from its suspended cells; and social insects live and work so intimately together in their hives or colonies that they may be said not to have an individual existence. Thomas concludes by calling into question the sharp differences between organelles and cells, organs and organisms, as we tend to perceive them. Nature, he implies, operates as a great homogeneous order in which humans may find their niche as the neurons and ganglia of an emerging global mind. This is the central theme upon which he expands in *The Lives of a Cell.*

In his title essay, "The Lives of a Cell," Thomas imagines the living cell as analogous to a bustling city, with its multitudes of complex functions and its organizational intricacy. Far from being a dead chamber, as Robert Hooke originally thought, the living cell is a paradox, both a single unit and a complex—an individual and a community. The organization of the cell is a metaphor for life on earth, for cells themselves are complex microbiotic ecosystems with many constituent parts. Our cells, Thomas remarks, may contain ecosystems as complex as Jamaica Bay. By extension, the image of the earth's biosphere as a vast, interconnected organism becomes the controlling metaphor for Thomas's book. As seen from space, the earth's atmosphere appears as a shimmering blue-white membrane, alive, tough, and impermeable. Thomas's speculations about the chemical stability and self-regulating mechanisms of the earth's atmosphere recall the controversial "Gaia hypothesis" advanced by James E. Lovelock and Lynn Margulis. They speculate that living organisms maintain a homeostatic balance and that the entire earth is in a sense "alive."[16] Lovelock believes that "the biosphere is a self-regulating entity with the capacity to keep our planet healthy by controlling the chemical and physical environment."[17] Johannes Kepler once advanced a similar notion of the earth as a living creature, Thomas reminds us. "In this immense organism, chemical signals might serve the function of global hormones, keeping balance and symmetry in the operation of various interrelated working parts, informing tissues in the vegetation of the Alps about the state of eels in the Sargasso Sea, by long, interminable relays of interconnected messages between all kinds of other creatures."[18] The Gaia theory represents symbiosis on a planetary level, with all levels of life operating in synchrony. It offers what Thomas calls elsewhere a new view of planetary evolution.

Organicism as Thematic Metaphor. In *The Lives of a Cell,* Thomas's essays are unified by the thematic analogy between the planet earth and the single cell, each incredibly intricate and mysterious, delicate and yet wonderfully resilient in its inner stasis. Thomas develops this organic metaphor in his title essay, "The Lives of a Cell," in his discussion of cellular symbiosis and his speculations about the evolutionary development of migrant prokaryocytes into the precursors of our eukaryotic cells. The astonishing uniformity of life, he argues, points to a single progenitor, an Ur-cell perhaps synthesized from amino acids in the great primal oceans of the young earth by the energy of a lightning bolt. If life has advanced through symbiotic partnerships to ever more complex forms, then perhaps cooperation is at least as important in nature as brute competition.

Thomas extends this analogy in "On Societies as Organisms," pointing to the dual nature of the social insects as both individuals and members of a social unit, or collective organism, the beehive or termite colony, and observing that on occasion even birds or fish join together in flocks or schools for their mutual benefit, behaving in some ways like a collective organism. Yet it is ironic that human beings, by far the most social creatures, are for the most part unaware of the interconnected, social dimension of their language and intelligence. Cooperative scientific research offers a neat paradigm, or model, of our social behavior, Thomas observes, particularly through the sharing of bits of research data in solving complex scientific problems beyond the ability of the individual researcher.

For this reason, Thomas finds the antisocial behavior of an African tribe called the Iks so disturbing, given his belief that human nature is basically cooperative and altruistic. In his essay "The Iks," Thomas responds to Colin M. Turnbull's *The Mountain People* (1972). Turnbull describes the utter dehumanization of an African tribe in less than three generations after being barred from the Kidepo National Park in Uganda where they had lived a nomadic life as hunters and gatherers. Forced to settle into subsistence farming on the barren uplands of East Africa, near the Sudanese border, the Iks were soon transformed into mean, selfish, brutish creatures with no love or concern for family or kin. Turnbull argues that our social virtues are not innate and that human nature can degenerate into competition for mere survival under conditions of drought and famine. For Turnbull, the Iks become a metaphor for the dehumanization and alienation of advanced industrial societies, while for Thomas they remain anomalies, social misfits who have lost their essential humanness under duress. In their extreme selfishness and egotism, they behave like communities, or worse yet, whole nations, squandering natural resources and polluting rivers and oceans with their effluent. According to Thomas, Turnbull's study points, not to the baseness of human nature, but to the fact that we have not yet learned how to be fully human in large groups, or ultimately, in nations. Given their divergent views of human nature, Thomas and Turnbull draw completely different interpretations from the example of the Iks.

In "An Earnest Proposal," Thomas points to the risks implicit in the alternative to organicism, the mechanistic metaphor, with its dangerously reductionistic view of life and its temptation to misuse science for lethal purposes. Ironically understating his case, he proposes that we defer any possible use of nuclear weapons and set our minds instead to the task of trying to understand thoroughly at least one other form of life. With Swiftian overtones, he modestly proposes that we set all of our computers and "practical men" to work studying *Myxotricha paradoxa,* a protozoan symbiont that lives in the digestive tract of Australian termites. Even if this project took a decade or more to complete, we owe it to ourselves to try and understand what we are about to destroy. Then the planning for nuclear war could resume. Thomas is willing to take his chances, since the project may be more complex than we imagine, as *Myxotricha* may turn out to be more elaborate and beautiful than we imagine. In Thomas's essay, this tiny, one-celled organism becomes an emblem for all of life: infinitely precious and irreplaceable. Through its symbiotic relationship with the termite, it demonstrates that all life is ultimately interconnected, a seamless web that cannot be torn. Thomas's organic vision of the unity of life contradicts the dark vision of Darwinian competition that justifies the nuclear strategy of mutually assured destruction. In short, if Thomas is correct, and *Myxotricha paradoxa* has anything to teach us, then the "practical men" and their nightmare vision of nuclear destruction are an aberration of nature: theirs is the wrong metaphor. By ignoring the role of cooperation in the natural world, they have drawn the wrong conclusions about human nature as well. Thomas earnestly hopes that the organic complexity of this "simple" protozoan will perplex the analytical ability of the most powerful computers and put off indefinitely the threat of nuclear war.

Language and Metaphor in Science. In his foreword to *Sagittal Section,* a collection of poems by Czechoslovakian poet and immunologist Miroslav Holub, Thomas commented that although scientists and poets appear to be engaged in different sorts of activities, they are actually involved in the "same kind of game," in finding "points of connection between things in the world which seem to most people unconnected."[19] Thomas seems to be implicitly acknowledging the importance of metaphor in scientific discourse, especially as a means of conveying abstractions or presenting new ideas. According to Lakoff and Johnson, in *Metaphors We Live By,* metaphors serve as part of a perceptual model, or linguistic framework (experiential gestalt), that we impose on reality. Metaphor is pervasive in everyday life and largely determines our conceptual system. "The essence of metaphor," they claim, "is understanding and experiencing one kind of thing in terms of another."[20] Descriptions of the physical world are impossible without images, and it is only a short step from images to metaphors. The more abstract the material, the more likely that metaphors will be employed to discuss it, especially in the choice of verbs. Scientific discourse is rife with metaphors, though they are not always recognized as such. Chemical atoms "like" to bond; physical forces "attract" or "repel"; electricity "flows"; and in biology, species "compete" and germs and viruses "invade" their hosts. The more abstract or theoretical the science, the more whimsical and imaginative the metaphors, with concepts in theoretical physics described in terms of billiards or Ping Pong balls and new particles given such unlikely names as "charm" or "quarks." In fact, the world of subatomic physics more nearly resembles that of James Joyce's *Finnegans Wake* or Lewis Carroll's *Alice in Wonderland* than that of the conventional physics laboratory. The metaphors we choose also subtly convey our feelings and attitudes toward the material we are describing, and we may convey unintended emotional connotations through the choice of inappropriate metaphoric comparisons.

Immunologist Fred Karush of the University of Pennsylvania has argued that in new fields such as immunology, the use of metaphors is inescapable, but it is important to recognize them as such so they are not misconstrued and do not take on the authority of scientific paradigms. Military metaphors seem to predominate in immunologic discourse, though scientists themselves are not inherently aggressive. It may be argued, Karush says, "that the only way we can name and characterize a new phenomenon is by reference to concepts with which we are already familiar, that is, by the use of analogy and metaphor."[21] Aristotle cautions that we must learn to be the master of our metaphors, and mastery is evident in Thomas's precise use of language in his essays. Too subtle to take his metaphors literally, Thomas deliberately employs a whole series of cooperative, nonviolent metaphors in his microbiological descriptions. His use of new and unexpected metaphors is part of his strategy for getting his readers to reexamine their scientific assumptions.

In the essay "Germs," Thomas characterizes our attitude toward disease as a modern kind of "demonology," in which we perceive bacteria as our adversaries. On the contrary, according to Thomas, "disease usually results from inconclusive negotiations for symbiosis, an overstepping of the line by one side or the other, a biologic misinterpretation of borders."[22] Most bacteria are not inherently pathogenic to their hosts and only become so when they produce endotoxin as a result of being themselves "diseased," perhaps through a viral infection. After all, microbes have as much to lose from being pathogenic as do their hosts. Often it is our body's own defense mechanisms that cause the symptoms of disease, by overreacting to the presence of endotoxins or to the information they carry, as in the case of some gram-negative bacteria.

Our phobia about germs is part of a cultural obsession with illness, Thomas argues in "Your Very Good Health," even though most of us are healthy most of the time. Thomas acknowledges that despite the advances of modern medicine, we are still beset by many diseases that we do not know how to control, but he insists that people do not contract major illnesses out of neglect or carelessness. On the contrary, he asserts, "most illnesses, especially the major ones, are blind accidents that we have no idea how to prevent."[23] In our neurotic preoccupation with illness, we pay too little attention to the built-in durability and resiliency of the human body. The great medical secret, known to most internists and their families, is that "most things get better by themselves."[24]

Our preoccupation with illness perhaps reflects a deeper cultural inability to accept the biological fact of death, Thomas argues in "The Long Habit." We evade the recognition of our mortality and project onto medicine unrealistic expectations for the extension of human life or even the eventual prospect of immortality. Thomas reminds us, however, that even the prevention or cure of most major illnesses would not alter the biological clocks in our bodies that determine our life span. Ours is a problem in attitude shaped by our wish to prolong our lives and our inability to visualize our own deaths. "The long habit of living indisposeth us to dying," he reminds us, quoting from Sir Thomas Browne's *Hydriotaphia, Urne-Buriall*.[25] Though we may think of death only as an abstraction, it is constantly occurring around us, as living creatures vanish into their progeny or as their organic remains are returned to the biosphere to be recycled and reconstituted in new forms of life. "Everything that comes alive seems to be in trade with something that dies, cell for cell," Thomas remarks in "Death in the Open."[26]

Given the universality and biological inevitability of death, Thomas points out the paradox of our culture's easy acceptance of mass death and nuclear annihilation in contrast to our inability to accept death on a personal scale—when it means us. Ironically, we hanker to go on living, even though our youth-oriented culture makes little provision for aging with dignity and tends to shunt the elderly aside. Old people live alone, fearful of being a burden to their children, and they die alone in hospitals, out of view. Our obsession with high-tech medical intervention to prolong life reflects the social view that death is shameful, whereas Thomas observes that from a strictly biological perspective, "dying is not such a bad thing to do after all."[27] It may even be a painless, calm, and peaceful detachment from life, he muses, one to prepare for with equanimity. A mortal injury may trigger the release of endorphins, or natural pain inhibitors, to ease the onset of death. Patients who have been brought back from near death report an experience of great peace and tranquility. The great mystery is how to account for the vanishing of consciousness, since Thomas believes that it is unlike nature to waste any major expenditure or concentration of energy.

In an analogous study, *Illness as Metaphor* (1978), Susan Sontag points out how out social perception of disease and death is conditioned by the metaphors we use. Using tuberculosis and cancer as primary examples, she argues that these diseases have become social metaphors, or tropes, with negative connotations. Thomas and Sontag seem to agree that illness has become a punitive metaphor in our culture, which burdens patients with guilt and responsibility for their illness. These metaphors seem to flourish especially where the pathogenesis of a disease is not fully understood, as with tuberculosis in the nineteenth century or cancer today, and tend to disappear once the causes of a disease are known and the illness becomes curable or preventable.

For example, the controlling metaphors in describing cancer and its treatment are drawn from the language of warfare—with malignant cancer cells "invading" the body, "colonizing" other tumor sites, resisting the body's immune "defenses," and "attacking" healthy cells.[28] Radiation therapy treatment also employs military terminology—with patients "bombarded" by X rays and injected with chemicals to "kill" cancer cells—almost as if the oncologists were waging war against the sick patient. Even the rhetoric of cancer research takes on the tone of a military campaign—with slogans about raising funds to "wage a war against cancer." Both Thomas and Sontag are wary of the distortions caused by such inappropriate metaphoric thinking, and they urge more care and restraint in the language we use in discussing illness. In the essay "On Magic in Medicine" in *The Medusa and the Snail,* Thomas returns to this topic of changing metaphors of disease and wellness and the ways in which these metaphors have shaped our understanding of disease.

Thomas himself is a keen student of language and has written about etymology, grammar, rules of punctuation, and the history of language, from both linguistic and sociobiological perspectives. He is acquainted with the structural linguistics based on the work of Lévi-Strauss and on that of Noam Chomsky and his colleagues at MIT, which hypothesize a genetic basis for grammar. Language building, Thomas theorizes, is the species-specific behavior that distinguishes humans as social animals, in much the same way that hive building or nest building is unique to bees or termites. Without the use of language, he believes, our minds would surely atrophy. In his opinion, language is alive and grows and mutates, with words functioning as the cells of the "organism." Or, to coin another metaphor, we build language the way termites use pellets to build a nest. As language grows and changes, it mutates and leaves behind etymological "fossils," which can be inferentially traced back, as in the case of the hypothetical ancestor of the present Indo-European language family.

Energy is encoiled within information, according to Thomas; but without the flexibility of language and the marvelous mutability of letters and words, that energy can be used only once. The beauty of language is in its capacity for ambiguity, for expressing nuances of meaning, as opposed to the rigidity of instinctual modes of communication. Ambiguity allows the freedom of choice and flexibility of human thought. The language of genetics might be compared to the genetics of language, Thomas muses, if we only knew more about each. Language, art, and music are essential to our social existence, as part of what he calls "the same universal, genetically determined mechanism."[29] In the essay "Ceti," he whimsically speculates about what information concerning Homo sapiens and life on earth we should be beaming out into interstellar space from *Voyagers* 1 and 2, and he decides that we should send the music of Johann Sebastian Bach as the best representation of what we are.

Communication between species is not limited to music or language, however. Thomas is also interested in olfactory communications and the biochemical messages that odors convey, especially as territorial markers or determinants of self. Olfactory receptors are also important for the establishment of symbiotic relations between different creatures, and there may be some link between the genes responsible for olfactory distinctions, those responsible for the cellular antigen markings for self, and those responsible for making immunologic responses. If we indeed have pheromones, like other mammals, we may be able to send out subtle emotional signals of our fear, stress, anger, or sexual receptiveness; we may even indicate our psychological makeup, since it has been reported that schizophrenic patients have a distinctive odor to their sweat.

The variety of animal sounds interests Thomas as well, and he writes about the new field of bioacoustics in "The Music of *This* Sphere." Nature is alive with creatures' noises, ranging from the clicking of termite mandibles and the ultrasonic squeaks of bats to deep-sea whale songs and the intricate improvisations of the wood thrush or the meadow lark. Thomas speculates that the urge to make music is a fundamental characteristic of terrestrial life, a reflection of the primeval transformation of the random chaos of matter into the orderly forms of life. Music may be part of the homeostasis of earth, the use of the sun's energy to convert matter into orderly and symmetrical forms, in opposition to entropy. The entire thrust of life, Thomas believes, is toward ever greater symbiotic order and complexity—a synergistic model—as the biosphere evolves toward a kind of global consciousness. Man's role, by implication, is not "to have dominion and control," in the biblical sense, but to be an indispensable part of the terrestrial ecosystem.

Skeptical of any claims of human uniqueness, biblical or biological, Thomas finds an uncanny resemblance between the behavior of social insects and the social behavior of man. In "Antaeus in Manhattan," he reflects on the fate of a colony of two million army ants from Central America, which died after being brought to New York and exhibited in a midtown gallery as part of a living art show. The show, "Patterns and Structure," entertained crowds of New Yorkers until the colony mysteriously sickened and died. Thomas speculates whimsically that like the giant Antaeus who lost his strength and was slain when Hercules lifted him off the ground, the ant colony could not survive for long after it was displaced from its native habitat to the cold drafts of a ground-floor Manhattan display window. Both ants and giants apparently need the support of Gaia, or Mother Earth.

Thomas's theory of symbiosis and his view of humans as social creatures lead him to question the notion of the autonomous self as a biological myth. In its place he offers a new metaphor of evolutionary symbiosis. We are all symbiotic assemblages, he believes, continually recycling the same chemicals and nutrients, and sharing in the same self-regulating planetary mechanism of the earth's biosphere, or what he calls in his concluding essay "the world's biggest membrane." This global, symbiotic perspective is carried forward into Thomas's second collection of essays, *The Medusa and the Snail*, which appeared in 1979. **Reception of *The Lives of a Cell*.** Thomas's editors at Viking Press were pleasantly surprised with the success of *The Lives of a Cell*, which was not expected to sell more than 10,000 copies. By 1979, *The Lives of a Cell* had sold over 250,000 copies and had been translated into eleven languages. It was particularly well received in some European countries, with the first Czechoslovakian edition of 20,000 copies, for instance, selling out within days and a Lewis Thomas anthology due to be published.[30] The initial American reviews were quite laudatory, with Joyce Carol Oates in the *New York Times Book Review* praising his "effortless, beautifully toned style" and observing that the book "might not yield its wisdom in a single reading."[31] She hails Thomas as one of a new breed of scientists who transcend the information they have absorbed from their disciplines to give us a new, unified vision. Oates commends Thomas for moving beyond antiquated nineteenth-century assumptions about the independence and isolation of man in nature to offer a graceful and gently persuasive vision of the interrelatedness of life. His optimism compares favorably, according to Oates, "with the gloomy romantic concepts of the isolation of the artist, the unnatural fact of man's language."[32]

John Updike, in a long *New Yorker* review, commends Thomas as a "lively, thoughtful writer" whose "willingness to see possibility where others see only doom is . . . tonic and welcome."[33] His only reservation concerns Thomas's altruistic view of nature, which Updike counters with the example of his well-fed cat returning each day with the corpses of field mice or baby rabbits, a dubious symbiotic relationship, at least for the prey. In contrast to Thomas, Updike may "cringe" at the "carnage and waste of the world," but he praises Thomas's "shimmering vision" of hope for "our increasingly crowded, irritable, depleted, de-institutionalized, and cannibalistic world."[34] Other encouraging reviews appeared in *Time* (22 July 1974) and *Newsweek* (24 July 1974), and Thomas's career as a popular essayist was underway. *The Lives of a Cell* won the National Book Award in 1974, earning the rare honor of being nominated both in the arts and the sciences categories. Thomas began to receive invitations to serve as a university commencement speaker as he became recognized as a major scientific spokesman. He would eventually earn more than fifteen honorary degrees and be elected as a fellow of the American Academy of Arts and Sciences. PBS-TV's program "NOVA" would feature him on one of its science documentary programs, and he would become the host of a projected but uncompleted science documentary series for the Public Broadcasting Service.[35]

The Medusa and the Snail: More Notes of a Biology Watcher

Thomas's first essay collection did so well for Viking Press that his editor, Elisabeth Sifton, urged him to consider putting together a second collection based on his *New England Journal of Medicine* columns and other sources.[36] This second collection of twenty-nine essays, *The Medusa and the Snail,* appeared in 1979. In it, Thomas expands upon his central theme of the symbiotic unity of nature, and he adds new selections on the science and technology of medicine, on medical education, and on miscellaneous topics ranging from Montaigne to the rules of punctuation. *The Medusa and the Snail* sold over 140,000 copies in hardcover edition, and its enthusiastic reception by reviewers resulted in a *Time* magazine cover story about Thomas in 1979.[37]

The Medusa and the Snail is a different kind of essay collection than *The Lives of a Cell,* at once more personal, more eclectic, and less exclusively scientific in its range of interests. There is a greater sense of authorial presence in these essays, with more personal anecdotes, a more consistent use of the first-person persona, and a more candid and self-revealing tone throughout the collection. In *The Medusa and the Snail,* Thomas also omitted the reference notes, with the list of technical articles, that he included at the end of *The Lives of a Cell,* recognizing that his essays were now aimed at a popular, rather than a scientific, audience. Though he was a master of the scientific style, Thomas was tired of writing for medical journals and wanted the freedom to write more informally for a more general audience. Ortega y Gasset's remark that "the essay is science minus the explicit proof" perhaps best articulates why Thomas was attracted to the open form of the familiar essay in seeking an alternative to the dense, flat, passive style of scientific journal writing. Part of this change in style may be attributed to Thomas's increased self-confidence as an essayist, after the enthusiastic critical response to his first book. The change may also be due to the influence of Montaigne, whose essays in the new Stanford edition, translated by Donald Frame, and published in 1965, Thomas confesses to have read closely over an eight-year period.[38] What Thomas learned from Montaigne was how to use the form of the brief familiar essay as a means of sharing his views on a wide variety of subjects with a circle of readers who are addressed as friends but not intimates. Thomas is intellectually candid but never emotionally confiding in tone. In this respect, he is calmer and cooler than Montaigne, more a disciple of pure reason and common sense, less volatile and less probing, more interested in the world of science than in himself.

The Thomas persona that emerges in *The Medusa and the Snail* is both personal and formal, willing to share his thoughts and insights but guarded about his feelings and his private life. After reading his essays, we know and respect him as a thinker, but he differs from Montaigne in that we have learned very little about Thomas as a human being, with all of his weaknesses and idiosyncrasies. The tone of his essays is a carefully modulated combination of intimacy and distance, friendliness and reserve, one that puts his readers at ease yet discourages easy familiarity. In his essays, Thomas does not dramatize or fictionalize his persona, as Loren Eiseley does, for example, but maintains an essay voice that seems to be an extension, rather than an alteration, of his personality.

It has been said that all essayists are egotists, but with Thomas, the emphasis seems to be more on the development of selected themes or topics and less on the essayist himself. Unlike Montaigne, who confides intimately in his readers, Thomas keeps a careful distance, maintaining a genial and engaging essay persona, sharing his thoughts and offering glimpses of his mind at work, so that the reader enjoys the experience (akin to good conversation) of listening to a first-rate mind thinking aloud. The key to understanding Thomas rests in his choice of engaging topics and in his rhetorical approach to his subjects, winning the reader's trust and respect both through his professional credentials and through his persona as a reasonable man.

Symbiosis as Metaphor. The title essay of Thomas's second book, "The Medusa and the Snail," describes the bizarre symbiotic relationship between two marine animals—a jellyfish and a nudibranch, or sea slug—found in the Bay of Naples. In a kind of hourglass pattern, the essay opens with the more comprehensive biological issues of the biological markers or boundaries of self, the uniqueness of individual organisms, and the ways in which organisms distinguish between self and nonself. Uniqueness is not a human quality alone but is shared among all biological organisms, down to the smallest bacteria, yet scientists know remarkably little about the sensing mechanisms that enable creatures to define themselves in their environment. Symbiotic relationships, or biological partnerships, may provide some answers to these questions, and Thomas uses the example of the medusa and the snail to raise these issues. He carefully traces the intermingled life cycle of these two organisms to demonstrate how cooperation between two unrelated species can create a partnership that benefits both organisms. How did such a bizarre and unlikely partnership arise, he wonders, and how did these organisms become so wholly dependent upon each other? This biological partnership becomes a trope, or metaphor, that Thomas develops throughout the book to emphasize the role of co-operation and collaboration as essential in human society as well as in nature. These are the traits that our complex, interdependent world needs, rather than individualism and competition, Thomas implies. He views humans essentially as social, rather than solitary, creatures; his interests are those of the city, the hospital, the committee; and his goal is to foster the kind of close, cooperative work that enables these human institutions to survive. The Thomas essay modulates between the human and the natural world, drawing examples from nature to support the kind of social values that Thomas believes are essential to human welfare. If he devalues individualism, it is because he believes that there is a greater human need at present for collaborative models of human behavior, ones that facilitate group problem-solving of complex social issues. The demands of our age would seem to encourage altruistic behavior, yet we've never been so individualistic or self-conscious of ourselves, Thomas muses, even though in nature, there's nothing unique about uniqueness.

Scientific reductionism may be the intellectual equivalent of rugged individualism, and in "The Tucson Zoo," Thomas emphasizes the need for a holistic perspective combining knowledge and wonder. He relates a personal anecdote of a zoo visit in which he was temporarily enchanted by the playful underwater behavior of the beaver and otter, so that his admiration for their graceful movements overwhelmed his physiological awareness of how their bodies function. For a moment his aesthetic response caused him to put aside his analytical, scientific interests. In an analogous manner, Thomas wonders whether, as social creatures, we may not be coded for altruistic behavior, waiting only for the right circumstances to elicit friendly cooperation with others. Solitary, selfish behavior is learned, he argues; at heart we hanker for friends and companions. Like the social insects, we are incomplete without others of our kind. Through language, we create an intricate social and cultural unity that transcends the individual.

In "The Youngest and Brightest Thing Around," an essay first given as a medical school commencement address at Columbia in 1978, this theme of man as a social animal is expanded to a vision of the unitary life of the planet. "All forms of life are connected," Thomas argues, and the earth itself is a vast, closed ecosystem, made up of numerous communities, from algal mats to modern cities. Viewed from space the earth resembles an enormous embryo, pulsating with life. We are a young species, ignorant of ourselves and of our role, though Thomas emphasizes that we are a compulsively social species, gifted with language, and that we "may be engaged in the formation of something like a mind for the life of this planet."[39]

The state of medicine is a favorite essay topic for Thomas, and in *The Medusa and the Snail,* four essays deal with various medical issues. "Magic is back again, and in full force," Thomas notes in "On Magic in Medicine," tracing the history of human misunderstanding of disease.[40] He laments the proliferation of quack remedies such as crash diets, copper bracelets, laetrile, meditation, yoga, and biofeedback, and he is just as skeptical that environmental factors or personal life-style have much to do with whether or not a person contracts cancer or heart disease. We just don't know enough yet about the real causes of these diseases, he cautions, so following the "seven healthy life habits" or eating a good breakfast to ward off the major degenerative diseases may have more to do with the power of suggestion than with medical fact. More basic research, skepticism, time, and patience are most needed, in Thomas's opinion, but in the meantime, magic provides the simple and readily comprehensible explanations that people crave.

In another essay, however, "On Warts," Thomas is ready to concede the power of hypnotic suggestion, at least in the removal of skin warts, which are initially caused by the body's response to viral infection. Thomas offers droll, whimsical praise of the powers of the unconscious, at least in responding to hypnotic suggestion, and he facetiously proposes a national research campaign to study the phenomenon.

Medical history is a bleak subject, Thomas notes in "Medical Lessons from History," because of the crude empiricism and sheer guesswork that passed for clinical treatment until a little over a century ago. To become a science, medicine had to pass through a period of therapeutic nihilism, when *all* treatment was doubted, and develop an accurate science of diagnosis and prognosis before physicians could be certain what they could actually cure. Medical progress depended on a foundation of basic biomedical research, leading to the development of the first antibiotics in the late 1930s. Thomas feels confident that the progress made in the treatment of infectious diseases will be repeated with the major degenerative diseases, but this will depend on the full understanding of the disease mechanisms involved and the discovery of the key mechanism that determines etiology for each disease. He is confident that all major human diseases are solvable human puzzles, so instead of dying of heart disease or cancer, we will "age away and wear out" like Oliver Wendell Holmes's wonderful one-horse shay.[41]

Thomas's essay "The Deacon's Masterpiece" uses Holmes's poem to create a modern myth about disease-free death as a gradual wearing out of the human body so that it finally collapses of old age, as a preclocked, genetically predetermined event. Medical progress will not bring about human immortality, Thomas cautions, but it could offer the prospect of disease-free lives and a full life span for the human race. The cloning of humans he dismisses as a fantasy, in "On Cloning a Human Being," because even if all the genes were identical, there would be no way to control all of the complex social and environmental factors that shape the human personality, so one's biological "twin" would still be a different person. Besides, the mechanism of cloning prevents the genetic diversity that has ensured the vigor of the species. Of course, there may also be a hidden agenda here in Thomas's countering Berkeley geneticist William Schockley's eugenics proposal to create a sperm bank of Nobel Prize winners in order to breed a race of superchildren.

In fact, a theme that runs throughout *The Medusa and the Snail* is the biological importance of error, mistake, and chance in bringing about favorable mutations and new adaptations. Error is opportunity for nature, Thomas asserts in "The Wonderful Mistake," extending the aphorism that to err is human, but "erring is biological as well." One of the marvels of the DNA molecule is this capacity for mutational change, a result of its chemical instability. Citing the etymological roots of the word *error* as meaning to "wander about, looking for something," Thomas concludes that perhaps it is the most appropriate word to describe the driving force behind evolutionary change.[42]

Mistakes are also the basis of creative human thought, Thomas asserts in "To Err Is Human," for without the fortuitous move based upon previous error, there would never be any human progress. Even our computers inherit this tendency for random errors, though we wrongly assume them to be infallible. As Thomas learned from his own research, what is important is not the error itself but how we respond to it.

Error is part of the price we pay for our freedom. The lower animals, lacking our complex brains, do not have this splendid capacity to err; they are limited to absolute infallibility. With choice comes the possibility of error; with the rigidity of instinct and patterned behavior comes the brittle perfection of the social insects.

Nor is absolute consistency and predictability a desirable trait in the human personality. In his humorous essay "The Selves," Thomas confesses to experiencing a number of different "selves," though fortunately not at the same time, he assures us. In a delightful analogy, he imagines the self as a kind of unruly committee chairman, moderating among the many contentious personalities striving to be heard. Like Emerson, Thomas eschews consistency and confesses to be embarrassed by the implication that having "more than a single self is a kind of disease."[43] Psychiatry would do well to counsel training in social etiquette, he mischievously suggests, to persuade these unruly selves to queue up and wait their turn. The only other way to quiet them is to play music, preferably Bach.

This mood of playful exuberance is carried over to Thomas's essays on language, where he indulges in his amateur hobby of linguistic and etymological speculation. In "On Etymons and Hybrids," he observes that most words naturally hybridize and change in the process of use and that etymons, or words that have retained their original meaning, are linguistically rare. Taking a cue perhaps from poet and etymologist John Ciardi, Thomas traces some of the unlikely origins of words like *poison, venom, virus,* and *chance.* Given the strange derivations of these words, Thomas facetiously wonders whether "rational management" and "scientific breeding" couldn't do better in creating new etymons. At times the style of his humor seems reminiscent of the early sketches he wrote for the *Princeton Tiger* as an undergraduate.

Satire and derision are the humorist's most powerful rhetorical weapons in ridiculing folly and promoting the claims of reason. Occasionally Thomas aims his barbs at some particularly likely target, as in his essay "On Transcendental Metaworry (TMW)." Though the target of his satire may now seem a bit dated, in the early 1970s the proponents of Transcendental Meditation made outrageous claims about the efficacy of their technique, expanding their cult into a whole industry of relaxation, with orientation sessions, instructional classes in relaxation, and custom-made mantras, all for a nice fee. There were even articles published in *Science* analyzing the benefits of "TM," as it was called. All of this was too much for Thomas, who found Transcendental Meditation an irresistible target for satire. His essay is a brilliant parody of the inflated claims and cult practices of TM, which he renames "Transcendental Metaworry," inverting its purposes from practicing relaxation to concentrating on worries. The tension from such concentrated worry will be so excruciating, Thomas asserts, that ordinary irritations will seem pleasurable in contrast.

An important distinction that Thomas draws in his essays is between science and pseudoscience. In "The Hazards of Science," he objects to the word *hubris* being used to describe the attitude of scientists, since the term implies that limits ought to be placed on scientific research, particularly in sensitive areas such as recombinant-DNA research. But Thomas flatly disagrees, arguing that we still know too little to be placing limits on scientific inquiry. Thomas believes that the desire to know is inherent in human nature and thus freedom of inquiry should not be limited, especially for emotional reasons. The real hubris is to assert that there are things we should not know. Who will make those choices and for what reasons?

"On Disease," the longest and most technical essay in *The Medusa and the Snail,* presents Thomas's theory of disease as a flawed response by the body's own immunologic system rather than the result of an invasion of foreign pathogens. Somehow, the endotoxins produced by certain pathogens stimulate an overreaction of the body's defense mechanisms, which themselves become the "disease," rather than the disease being the consequence of bacterial or viral infection. Drawing from his work in experimental pathology, Thomas discusses the etiology of meningitis and diphtheria, finding in each case none of the aspects of a conventional predator-prey relationship that used to be assumed for infectious disease. Modern research has shown that the germ theory of disease needs considerable revision. Most bacteria and viruses are innocuous to humans, and disease actually presumes the breakdown of a symbiotic relationship between microbe and host. Even when bacteria are pathogenic, as with diphtheria, it is because they produce exotoxins, excretions that are harmful to the host. The toxin-cell reaction is a two-way relationship of great intimacy, involving the recognition and precise match of the toxin and the cell, as though the toxin were a normal participant in the cellular metabolism. Most germs, however, are not our natural enemies. As Thomas observes, "germs are all around us; they comprise a fair proportion of the sheer bulk of the soil, and they abound in the air."[44] Beneficial bacterial flora live in our intestinal tracts and assist in the breakdown of essential nutrients. Other bacterial colonies live on the root nodules of legumes and assist in the conversion of atmospheric nitrogen. Soil bacteria are essential in recycling mineral nutrients through the decay of dead organic matter. The vast majority of bacteria are innocuous or helpful. Thomas points out that if mitochondria and chloroplasts are regarded as the descendants of free-living bacteria, then the vast majority of bacteria on earth today are essential symbionts in the photosynthetic, or oxidative, cycles of other organisms. Without them we could not exist. In comparison, the number of bacteria whose toxins are pathogenic to humans seems inconsequential. Thomas is skeptical of the need to quarantine returning astronauts or spacecraft because of the threat of infection from alien germs, since disease seems to be the result of a long and intimate relationship between pathogen and host.

"To philosophize is to learn to die," Montaigne observed in his *Essays,* and Thomas demonstrates his philosophical composure in his essay "On Natural Death," in which he speculates that natural endorphins may actually ease the pain of the terminally injured. He quotes from Montaigne's own experience of a near-fatal horseback riding accident, in which he found himself drifting off into a peaceful languor and gently letting go of consciousness. Pain is only useful for avoidance, Thomas asserts, and the body has mechanisms for suppressing unbearable pain when there is no hope for recovery.

Thomas and Montaigne.   In his essay "Why Montaigne Is Not a Bore," Thomas pays tribute to Montaigne as a great humorist and moralist, and a keen student of human nature. Thomas enjoys Montaigne's candid self-appraisal, his puzzlement over his inconsistencies and weaknesses, and his cheerful acceptance of his personal limitations. For Thomas, Montaigne's essays project the quality of good conversation, and through them the author reaches out to his readers as a friend, confiding revelations of himself that the reader shares as well. Montaigne's essays offer a candid self-appraisal that never becomes self-approval, and through his clear self-understanding he speaks to the universal human condition.

The range and variety of Thomas's interests and the persistence of his curiosity bring to mind Montaigne, since both writers embody those qualities of mind, temperament, and education that enable them to find something of interest in virtually anything. Just as Montaigne's essays are a record of his learning, so almost every page of a Thomas essay deals in some way with education: not professional pedagogy, but the intellectual qualities that enable a person to think and learn for himself.

Indeed, as one reviewer notes, "if Montaigne had possessed a knowledge of twentieth-century biology, he would have been Lewis Thomas."[45]

Along with Montaigne, Thomas shares insatiable curiosity and absolute frankness and honesty. His desire is to communicate with a broad, general audience and share with them his temperamental optimism and careful habits of thinking cultivated by a lifetime of medical research. Like Montaigne, he uses natural, everyday language in order to put the most abstract scientific ideas in the clearest and simplest terms. Both writers are fond of a discursive style that enables them to move unobtrusively from topic to topic. Even Thomas's choice of essay titles (in his use of the tentative "On . . .") resembles that of Montaigne. From his own field of cellular immunology, Thomas often makes broad leaps of analogy from microcosm to macrocosm, from the workings of the cell to the ecological organization of the earth itself. Here he finds a nascent collective "mind" gradually emerging, with mankind serving as the neural network of this new planetary consciousness. Such thoughts are heady stuff, but Thomas has other equally startling predictions to offer as well, such as his confidence that the cause of cancer will prove to be a cellular "switch" rather than a series of viral, environmental, or hereditary factors.

Unlike Montaigne, however, Thomas is more interested in the world around him than in himself or the vagaries of his mind. Aside from an occasional personal anecdote, he does not engage as much in the kind of self-revealing reveries or confessions that have made Montaigne's *Essays* so endearing to generations of readers. Instead, Thomas is more matter-of-fact and impersonal, focusing primarily on the subject at hand rather than self-consciously catching himself in the act of thinking or reflecting upon a given topic. As a result, Thomas loses some of the leisureliness and charm of Montaigne's speculations, but he compensates with a directness and incisiveness that enables him to get to the heart of an issue and explore it within the constraints of the short-essay form. Whether Thomas offers as full a personal philosophy or portrait of human nature as does Montaigne is debatable, but he offers a reassuring voice of scientific hope and optimism at a time of widespread public mistrust of science and doubts about our immediate and long-term prospects. As a public spokesman for medical science, he provides a compelling model of clear writing and incisive thinking.

What Thomas shares with Montaigne is the generic assumption that the essay presents a lyrical and creative ordering of ideas—a careful rhetorical arrangement that still conveys the illusion of spontaneity and improvisation. Like Montaigne, Thomas sometimes uses self-deprecating humor to win his readers' confidence, but this persona is largely a rhetorical posture, derived from an authority so confident of itself that it can afford to be casual and familiar, even confidential with the reader. Thomas's humorous irony can take the form of a bemused bewilderment with the complexity of modern science or with the intricacies of modern technology, but it also allows him the freedom to present complex ideas clearly and simply by assuming that the reader shares his confusion and would appreciate his attempts at clarification. The ironic humor shared by Thomas and Montaigne also emerges from their deliberate strategy of presenting serious ideas in a casual, almost offhand manner. It may also result from the skeptical and tentative stance of each essayist—the stance of a mature, intelligent, and critical mind taking its measure of the world of ideas. The shared confidence of essayist and reader defines the realm of the familiar essay and accounts for its perennial appeal, for Montaigne's age and our own, both periods of cultural change in which traditional explanations were suspect and new knowledge demanded new formulations. The essay in its purest form is thus a "trying out" of new ideas, an attempt to articulate new interpretations of a new reality.

The Essay and the Art of the Fugue

Through his appreciation of Bach, Thomas became interested in the analogy between the fugue and the essay form, particularly in the ability of each medium to generate several different motifs or ideas simultaneously and then develop each in counterpoint. In fact, this is what Thomas seems to be doing with the major themes or ideas that he introduces in his first two essay collections. He throws out a half-dozen brilliant insights or ideas in an essay and then returns to them at a later point to elaborate or qualify an important idea. A great admirer of Bach's music, Thomas makes a number of allusions in his essays to the *Brandenburg Concertos,* the *St. Matthew's Passion,* and the *Art of the Fugue.* He often listened to cassette tapes of Bach's music late into the night when he was involved with some interesting project. Just as Bach used the contrapuntal style of theme and variation in his fugues, in which a theme or melody is introduced in one voice and then imitated by other voices in close succession, so Thomas used an analogous method of composition in his essays, presenting several different ideas simultaneously. The analogies between music and thinking intrigued

Thomas as well.[46] He was fascinated by musical composition because he believed that it externalized the thought processes of the brain—that a musical score represents the thought processes and emotions of the composer set in time. Music immortalizes the mind of the composer, though the score is only a blueprint for the performance. In "On Thinking about Thinking," he likens one of Bach's great oratorios, the *St. Matthew's Passion,* to the sound of the mind itself thinking—the whole nervous system at work.

What the musical analogy suggests is an insight into Thomas's methods as a lyrical essayist, especially in regard to his repetition of certain key themes that he presents in more than one essay. Just as the baroque composer used theme and counterpoint as a way of developing a musical idea, Thomas uses a fugal pattern of argument to advance a claim or examine a new or startling concept from various perspectives. This repetition may also be a result of his improvisational method of composition. In one recent interview, he commented that he does not begin with a preconceived thesis or outline but instead writes fairly quickly and intuitively, allowing the form to find itself, depending on his topic.[47] Typically, he will open with a controversial assertion, which invites his readers to reexamine his topic from a new perspective, and then he develops his insights using rhetorical patterns of paradox, enigma, irony, antithesis, inversion, hyperbole, or compression to inform, to explain, and ultimately to persuade us of the validity of his position. Even in his most daring speculations, Thomas maintains the persona of a reasonable man, but one who is willing to challenge the conventional interpretation of an issue in order to advance our understanding. The result is to create the illusion of Thomas thinking aloud, to capture the spontaneous creativity of creative thought as perhaps only the familiar essay allows a writer to do. Thinking is like Brownian movement, Thomas asserts, a purposeful randomness, and his infatuation with the fugal form allows his lyrical essays to approach the condition of music.

A Philosophy of Nature

As John Updike noted in his review of *The Lives of a Cell,* beneath his science Thomas is at heart a mystic who seeks patterns of unity and coherence in nature.[48] His faith in the unity of the cosmos goes beyond the observable, as he makes clear in his allusions to the fourteenth-century mystic Julian of Norwich. As a philosopher of nature, Thomas does not hesitate to ask the most fundamental and difficult questions, the ultimately metaphysical questions about the essence, destiny, and purpose of man, and about how humans fit into the natural order of life. A monist at heart, he is certain that such an order exists and that it will eventually be discovered. In an uncollected essay published in 1980, "On the Nature of Nature," Thomas offers a concise statement of his philosophy. Here he takes the "long view" in considering planetary evolution and in looking for continuities in the progression of life. Modern science is still in its infancy, he believes, and does not have enough information to understand the basic unity of life. Viewed from space, the earth appears like an immense embryo in which the entire biosphere functions as a closed ecosystem.

The system works by interchange, by trading among parts, by collaboration. Creatures accommodate to each other, move to one side to make room, live by rules. Symbiosis is the fundamental mechanism that makes the System viable. Without interliving, the place could never work. The most eminent, spectacular symbionts of all are, of course, the chloroplasts and mitochondria, tapping the sun and making use of it, in aid of all the rest of us. But there are others, everywhere you look. Every living form is engaged, one way or another, in feeding other forms. There is a kind of mutual responsibility at work, holding all the parts together, weathering out the tremendous cyclic changes that occur in the earth's morphogenesis, surviving one cataclysm after another and emerging after each looking more splendid than ever.[49]

In a fundamental way, nature is ourselves and we have become nature, so that our understanding of nature reflects our understanding of ourselves. But this does not mean that we are in charge. We are part of a larger order of planetary evolution, which we do not understand very well yet. If we mistakenly find nothing but violence and conflict in the natural world, then we will assume the same of human nature, since we project our metaphors onto nature. For this reason, Thomas's understanding of symbiosis, with its collaborative natural communities of organisms that signal, negotiate, adapt, form partnerships, and co-operate, offers a refreshing view of the natural world. A basic theme that runs throughout Thomas's work is the paradoxical relationship in nature between individual uniqueness and the collective biological unity of life on earth. In science, as Thomas has observed, for every truth there is an opposite and complementary truth. This is especially true of the question of biological identity. Each of us is genetically unique, yet through the myriads of symbiotic relationships from the cellular level to the species, we are all interrelated, composite organisms. We all share the same basic organic materials—oxygen, carbon, nitrogen, hydrogen, and phosphorus—that are continuously recycled throughout the biosphere. We are all ultimately dependent on chloroplasts, which store solar energy through photosynthesis, and mitochondria, which help metabolize the food energy in our cells. None of us really owns or occupies ourselves. Instead, we are owned and occupied, rented by microorganisms that assist our metabolism by performing vital functions within our cells and organs. In "On Probability and Possibility," Thomas observes that "the whole dear notion of one's own Self—marvelous old free-willed, free-enterprising, autonomous, independent, isolated island of a Self—is a myth."[50] With lower orders of life, such as sponges, it is often difficult to tell where the individual cells end and the organism begins. It is possible to reduce the sponge to its component cells by squeezing a piece of the sponge into salt water, yet if the cells are held together in suspension long enough, they will begin to regroup into a composite organism. Though discrete entities, marine algae show a tendency to group together in vast colonies, or mats, which are stratified in different colors according to variety. And though of the same species, different varieties of sea anemones are able to fend off genetically unlike intruders as they compete for space in which to feed on the seabed. Even bacteria show some signs of individuality and can react purposively in response to light, magnetic, or heat stimuli. This biological question of the boundaries between self and other becomes an important theme that is carried over from *The Lives of a Cell* to *The Medusa and the Snail* and Thomas's later works.

Chapter Four

Notes of a Science-Watcher: A Medical Memoir and More Essays

In a recent article in the *American Scholar,* Jeremy Bernstein commented that there are three reasons to teach science to the nonscientist: curiosity, technological bewilderment, and technological necessity.[1] Thomas would probably agree with Bernstein's assessment and add a few motivations of his own: the desire to communicate the fun of doing science and the need to share the scientist's recognition of the limits of scientific understanding and the awareness of how much is yet to be learned about nature. This is where science education should begin, not with masses of facts, formulas, and data, but with the frank recognition of how little is known about the natural world, for in Thomas's opinion, "it is the very strangeness of nature that makes science engrossing."[2] Thomas's move from the *New England Journal of Medicine* to *Discover* magazine was an implicit acknowledgment that the main audience for his essays was, after all, composed of nonscientists.

Starting in 1980, Thomas began writing for the monthly science magazine *Discover* at the invitation of Andrew Heiskell, chairman of the board of Time-Life and a fellow board member with Thomas on the Harvard University Board of Overseers. The editors of *Discover* had decided that they could use some reflective essays to balance their format, and Thomas was mentioned as someone to approach. After being contacted by Henry Grunwald, the editor in chief, and Leon Jaroff, the founding editor of *Discover,* Thomas agreed to give it a try, and he became a regular columnist for the next seven years, through 1986. He began by writing a column a month for *Discover,* though his output later dropped to only two or three essays a year.

In 1980, Thomas retired as president and chief executive officer of Sloan-Kettering, although he remained there in the largely honorary role of chancellor until 1983. His reduced administrative responsibilities gave him more time to devote to writing. He also closed down his laboratory in the summer of 1981, though he continued to work with colleagues at Yale on the problem of Alzheimer's disease. He spent the fall of 1981 as a visiting fellow at Clare Hall, Cambridge University, conducting studies of the scrapie, or slow viruses, which cause delayed symptoms of brain damage. In 1983, he was named university professor at the State University of New York at Stony Brook, a flexible appointment that allowed him to work as he chose with the medical, biology, or English faculties without any formal teaching obligations. His primary responsibilities at Stony Brook were to lecture occasionally and to chair a university committee charged with reviewing all of the life-science courses on campus and strengthening them wherever possible. The Stony Brook appointment gave him more time to spend at his weekend home in East Hampton, on eastern Long Island, which he and his wife, Beryl, enjoyed as an escape from Manhattan. Even after his retirement, his advisory work with the Harvard and Princeton boards of trustees kept him commuting between Boston and New Jersey. He also lectured occasionally, such as when his membership on the Advisory Council of the National Institute on Aging brought him to Brookhaven Laboratory in 1984 to give a talk entitled "The Odds on Normal Aging."

Spending more time in the Hamptons after his retirement allowed Thomas the leisure to write in the bright new studio recently added to his cottage. Though he turned seventy in 1983, he maintained a busy writing schedule, finishing a medical memoir and a third collection of essays, giving several extended public lectures, and collaborating on a new, limited edition of his poems, with illustrations by his East Hampton neighbor Alfonso Ossorio. Unfortunately, an early morning fire in October 1987 largely destroyed the Thomas's East Hampton home, resulting in the loss of many of his precious books, manuscripts, and records. His daughter accompanied Dr. Thomas on a trip to Europe in the winter of 1988 while the house was being rebuilt.

Thomas continued to receive honors and tributes after his retirement. By 1984, he had been granted over twenty honorary degrees. He was invited to deliver the annual Harvard Phi Beta Kappa oration in 1980, which he entitled "On the Uncertainty of Science."[3] That same year, he won a special award in literature from the American Academy and Institute of Arts and Letters and the Woodrow Wilson Award for distinguished alumni service from his alma mater, Princeton University. A special symposium on "Infection, Immunity, and the Language of

Cells" was held in his honor at the New York University Medical Center on 22 November 1982, with the proceedings published in a special commemorative issue of the journal *Cellular Immunology*.[4] The affair was something of a homecoming for Thomas, with the talks organized and later edited by Thomas's good friend and colleague Dr. H. Sherwood Lawrence, a distinguished immunologist at the NYU School of Medicine. A year later, in 1983, Thomas received the Kober Medal from the Association of American Physicians, at its annual banquet held in Washington, D.C., from 29 April to 2 May. A special citation recognized Thomas's contributions "to the progress and achievement of the medical sciences or preventive medicine."[5]

In honor of Thomas's seventieth birthday, on 7 December 1983 the Board of Directors of Time Inc. and the Scientists' Institute for Public Information (SIPI) threw a gala birthday party for Thomas in the Tower Suite of the Time-Life Building. Over two hundred guests attended the lavish dinner and watched a special multimedia program about Thomas's career narrated by Walter Cronkite. After listening with bemusement to several long-winded personal tributes, Thomas was asked to stand and offer some impromptu remarks to the guests, but he demurred, saying that it was already late in the evening and everyone had already heard enough, so he simply thanked everyone who had made the affair possible and left it at that.

Perhaps the most impressive honor Thomas received was when Princeton decided to name its new $29 million molecular biology facility after him. The Lewis Thomas Laboratory, the first building at Princeton named after a living alumnus, was dedicated on 18 April 1986. The building was made possible by a generous $10 million gift from Thomas's former classmate and Princeton trustee, Laurance Rockefeller. The innovative layout of the building's labs, seminar rooms, and lounge areas was designed to facilitate some of Thomas's ideas about collaborative teamwork in scientific research. The interior space was designed to integrate teaching and research and to encourage interdisciplinary co-operation among the biology, chemistry, and physics departments. The molecular biology program at Princeton was just three years old, and its staff hoped that the fine new research facility would serve as a recruiting tool to attract new faculty. At the building's dedication, Thomas joked that "it's an unnerving experience to become a Princeton building."[6] At a dinner afterward, he delivered an address entitled "High Hopes for Princeton."

The Youngest Science

Thomas's administrative and research activities lessened as he neared retirement, and he became increasingly interested in medical history. He wrote a long profile for *Esquire* magazine about the pioneering biologist Oswald Avery, whose work on pneumococcus bacteria at the Rockefeller Institute for Medical Research in the 1930s and early 1940s contributed to the discovery of DNA.[7] Given these interests, it is not surprising that Thomas was persuaded to undertake a medical memoir for the Alfred P. Sloan Foundation as the third title in their series on the lives of distinguished modern scientists. The first two titles were Freeman Dyson's *Disturbing the Universe* and Peter Medawar's *Advice to a Young Scientist*. Thomas, who had been used to working with the short-essay genre, found the extended narrative form more difficult, according to his editor, and his manuscript went through a number of revisions. *The Youngest Science: Notes of a Medicine-Watcher* is a curiously uneven book, one that begins as autobiography and then gradually becomes more impersonal as the later chapters lapse back into essay form.

The scientific memoir itself is a strange, mixed genre, as both Peter Medawar and Erwin Chargaff have noted, though each has written his own memoir. The genre itself is not as personally revealing as autobiography nor as dramatically compelling as biography. "The difficulties facing a man trying to record his life are great," notes Erwin Chargaff, and "they are compounded in the case of scientists."[8] Ideally, the scientific memoir is the portrait of a life in a profession, the story of the growth of a profession, or a subspecies of intellectual autobiography. At its best, it may capture something of the climate of the times or the excitement of major scientific discoveries, but at its worst, it can be dull or self-promotional. As Peter Medawar comments in *Pluto's Republic:* "The lives of scientists, considered as Lives, almost always make dull reading. . . . It could hardly be otherwise. Academics can only seldom lead lives that are spacious or exciting in a worldly sense. They need laboratories or libraries and the company of other academics. Their work is in no way made more cogent by privation, distress or worldly buffetings. Their private lives may be unhappy, strangely mixed up or comic, but not in ways that tell us anything special about the nature or direction of their work."[9]

These inherent difficulties in the genre may have resulted in the curiously mixed perspective of Thomas's memoir, which tries to convey both a personal portrait and the story of the growth of modern medicine.

Thomas places his own career within the larger framework of the emergence of modern medicine since the 1930s, but neither receives the attention it deserves. Thomas has enjoyed a distinguished career, and he is appropriately modest about his many successes, but he presents only the outward events of his life without any of the inner drama, so as personal narrative it seems flat and uncompelling. He does not tell the story of a great scientific discovery, as in the case of James Watson's *The Double Helix,* which recounts the scientific competition that led to the discovery of the structure of the DNA molecule; nor does he provide a reflective personal philosophy, as does Rene Dubos's *A God Within;* nor does his memoir offer the personal vibrancy and lucidity of Peter Medawar's *Memoir of a Thinking Radish.* Though Thomas has expressed his admiration for another recent scientific memoir, Erwin Chargaff's *Heraclitean Fire: Sketches from a Life before Nature,* his own memoir lacks the sardonic wit and brilliance of Chargaff's book, which seems much more poised and self-assured than Thomas's memoir.[10]

Webster's Third New International Dictionary defines memoir as "a personal narrative; an autobiographical account often anecdotal or intimate whose focus of attention is usually on the persons, events or times known to the writer." In the scientific memoir, these events need a clear perspective or point of view, since they are usually not inherently dramatic. Thomas, however, writes as an insider, and he is not inclined to be critical of his profession or of scientific research in general. The more research the better, he asserts, but that attitude begs some important moral and ethical questions concerning the applications of biomedical research and technology.

Medicine has become a science in the past generation, and this change is all to the good, according to Thomas. But unfortunately it is not yet fully a science, nor does it remain wholly an art. Thomas confesses that as a meliorist, he views these changes as necessary and good, but public perceptions of the new medical technology are quite mixed. Many questions have been raised about the ethics and propriety of recombinant-DNA research, genetic engineering, test-tube conceptions, and other biomedical innovations that seem to threaten the sanctity of life, as well as the status of the medical profession itself. As Paul Starr argues in *The Social Transformation of American Medicine,* the doctor-patient relationship has suffered in recent years and physicians are perceived as curt, distant, clinical, and indifferent, interested primarily in maintaining lucrative practices and unwilling to devote much time to their patients.[11]

Writing as an insider, Thomas seems to lack critical perspective on these issues, or else he chooses not to deal with them.

The twenty-two chapters in *The Youngest Science* are divided between personal reminiscence and medical history, with the early chapters depicting Thomas's Flushing childhood and the influence of his parents on his decision to pursue a medical career, and the later chapters describing his medical research and administrative experiences. Aside from the poignant sketches of his father, a respected family physician who later became a surgeon, and of his mother, a skilled nurse and woman of strong character, Thomas discusses little in the way of formative influences. In fact, his memoir is more notable for what it omits than for what it mentions. What about his early reading, his schooling, his college years, his teachers or other role models, his childhood friends or brothers and sisters? Scarcely a word is mentioned. Nor does he say much about his courtship and marriage to his wife, Beryl (née) Dawson, whom he credits with much of his success, or about his three daughters. While Thomas wisely avoids the gossipy tone of Watson's *The Double Helix,* he could have risked telling us a bit more about his personal life. In short, there is remarkably little here to enliven this memoir with the domestic touches, personal insights, or individual, cultural, or intellectual tastes that would help to flesh out a self-portrait. Thomas is notably circumspect in this memoir, and even a scientific autobiography is not the genre to choose for someone who wants to protect his privacy. As a result, his memoir lacks the warmth and charm of a book like Milton J. Slocum's *Manhattan Country Doctor,* or the critical perspective of Melvin Konner's *Becoming a Doctor,* although of course Thomas's career has been in biomedical research and not in general practice.

Despite the overall lack of narrative continuity, several chapters stand out in Thomas's memoir, such as "Nurses," a tribute to the nursing profession, and "Illness," Thomas's account of his own experience as a patient. In his sixties, Thomas was hospitalized, first, for what turned out to be arteriovenous anomaly and, subsequently, for a torn knee cartilage and a dislocated and fractured shoulder. His series of hospitalizations reminded him of what it was like to be a patient and taught him to put his trust in his attending physician, since Thomas confessed that he didn't really want to know what was happening to him or to take responsibility for his own medical decisions. These matters, he felt, were better left with the medical specialists. In a subsequent essay in *Late Night Thoughts on Listening to Mahler's Ninth Symphony,* "My Magical Metronome," he writes of his experience in being fitted with an electronic pacemaker and how he came to value the "halfway" medical technologies that he had formerly criticized. These incidents, although interesting in themselves, might have taken on additional value if they were not isolated sketches but part of a continuous narrative in which Thomas reflected on the personal experience of aging from a physician's perspective. Thomas's instinct, though, is to conceal rather than to reveal, and as a result the dry and impersonal tone of *The Youngest Science* better suits a medical history than a personal memoir.

Whatever its autobiographical limitations, *The Youngest Science* presents a cogent history of the many transformations in American medicine since World War II. Thomas's account may be read as an extended comparison between the medical practices of his father's generation, with its limited efficacy and therapeutic nihilism, and the curative possibilities made available with the discovery of antibiotics and the new medical technologies developed during the war. Whereas the practice of medicine had formerly been primarily diagnostic, with the emphasis on explanation of the patient's problem rather than treatment or cure, it now became more therapeutic, as physicians discovered that they had a powerful array of drugs and techniques at their disposal. With the advent of a new, scientific medicine, the social status of the profession suddenly rose, and physicians no longer had to struggle to make a living. As medicine became big business, many doctors became highly successful entrepreneurs. Thomas's father struggled to pay his bills with his family practice, made house calls at all hours of day or night, and never expected to become wealthy by practicing medicine. Thomas recalls that in a questionnaire sent out to Harvard medical school graduates in 1937, the average income for ten-year graduates was thirty-five hundred dollars and only seventy-five hundred dollars for twenty-year graduates.[12] The status of medicine began to change after the war, but there were some trade-offs, as Stephen Jay Gould has noted, between heart and efficiency, between personal attention to patients and efficacy of care.[13] Physicians no longer had to rely on the placebo power of their nostrums or on the unpredictable healing power of suggestion. Now physicians could intervene in new and powerful ways to cure a wide array of infectious or degenerative diseases. With the new power and prestige of medicine, however, came a new kind of practitioner, one who was sometimes perceived (rightly or wrongly) as being more interested in wealth and status than in healing people. What had once been a humane healing profession was becoming a powerful and prestigious biomedical science. But in the public's eye, something had gone dreadfully wrong with this new generation of physicians. Primary patient care was increasingly relegated to nurses, who resented the implication that their work was of secondary importance, and as medical costs skyrocketed, malpractice suits increased and the public began to lose confidence in high-tech medicine. The new breed of physician became a kind of high-powered specialist, who was often accused of being too busy to listen, more interested in treating the ailment than the patient. As the stakes for entering the profession increased, the competition to enter medical schools became cutthroat, and undergraduate education suffered as premedical students became increasingly grade conscious and refused to take humanities electives. Thomas has talked elsewhere about abolishing the premedical curriculum and reforming medical school admission practices, but the problem is that medicine is no longer perceived as a humane profession but has become part of the huge health-care services industry.[14]

There is no doubt that these trends will continue as medicine becomes increasingly scientific. With the new advances in pathology, diagnosis will become more of a science than an art. New methods of computer analysis will supplement traditional blood tests and X rays, and the days of artful guesswork in the laboratory or of diagnosis by process of elimination will be over. New techniques like DNA probes will permit accurate diagnosis of viral infections by identification of viral proteins. Pathologists will probably play a more important role in primary medicine in the early detection and treatment of major illnesses. These are the kinds of changes that Thomas welcomes and that make him so confident about the future of biomedical science. As Jeremy Bernstein has commented, medicine is no longer a laying on of hands but the reading of signals from machines.[15]

In Thomas's comparison of his own medical career with that of his father, much of his attention is devoted to medical research and to the research problems and medical hypotheses that have intrigued him. These chapters read like separate essays rather than a continuous narrative of Thomas's career, although, to his credit, he is excited about new ideas and manages to convey that excitement to his readers. Contrary to prevailing opinion, Thomas believes that cancer may have a common etiology, arising from the malfunction of a genetic "switch" ordinarily regulated by the immune system. The clues to its understanding may lie in the study of embryology and the immune system. His immunological surveillance theory of cancer has been promoted by Sir MacFarlane

Burnet, with Thomas never receiving full credit for his brilliant but as yet unproved intuition.[16]

More recently, Thomas's theory of disease as the result of a dysfunction of host mechanisms has been confirmed in the research on AIDS, in which the initial viral infection leads to a sudden loss of immune reactivity on the part of the body's lymphocytes. Associated with this loss of the normal immune defenses is the high incidence of otherwise rare cancers such as Kaposi's sarcoma and non-Hodgkin's lymphomas, as well as a variety of rectal, gastric, and skin cancers. The AIDS virus somehow seems to trick the body's immune system into relaxing its normal defenses, with suppressed T-helper cells and overactive T-suppressor cells. Ironically, the AIDS epidemic has led Thomas to revise his optimistic forecasts that the major infectious diseases of mankind were being eliminated and would soon vanish entirely as threats to human health. With the worldwide epidemic of AIDS and the appearance of Legionnaires' disease and Lyme arthritis, Thomas fears that the battle against infectious disease is far from won and that in fact, new diseases may appear, unpredictably, at any time. There is still much research to be done in immunology and microbiology.[17]

Other chapters in *The Youngest Science* describe Thomas's elegant clinical studies of endotoxin, the toxic substance retained within the body of pathogenic bacteria, and of mycoplasmas, the smallest known free-living organisms. Intermediate between bacteria and viruses, these mammalian parasites are often the agents of inflammation and degenerative disease. Thomas hypothesizes that endotoxins provide a working model for one theory of disease: "that disease can result from the normal functioning of the body's own mechanisms for protecting itself, when these are turned on simultaneously and too exuberantly, with tissue suicide at the end."[18] Mycoplasmas may trigger inappropriate responses from the host's immune system by mimicking the host's own cells. They make people sick by altering the immune response. Through their biological mimicry, they are not recognized by the host as foreign organisms. As in the case of rheumatoid arthritis, they stimulate the production of antibodies to the host's own cells and cause the host's immune system to attack its own cells, although why they do this is not known.

Thomas has also been fascinated by the physiology of odors as a clue to biological identity or selfhood. He believes there may be a connection between biochemical tagging by one's own genes and tissue-graft rejection, which is caused by the immune system's recognition and rejection of foreign substances. These immunologic markers of self are present in all skin cells and trigger the rejection of skin grafts. Thomas's work has led him to experiment with police dogs, which have the ability to distinguish and track the particular scents of individual persons, and with lines of genetically inbred mice, whose mating behavior shows that they can distinguish individuals different in only a single H-2 gene.[19] Tracking mice can smell out this minute genetic difference, which is present in mouse urine. The odorant also causes pregnancy blocking, the spontaneous abortion of newly impregnated females placed in the same cage with a strange male. Thomas was surprised to learn that Scotland Yard police dogs can also scent out this one-gene (H-2) difference among congenetically bred mice. He speculates that specially trained dogs might one day be able to scent out histocompatible donors for tissue or organ transplants. Nor is this self-marking and tissue-recognition response unique to mammals: it occurs in sponges and corals as well.

Thomas has spent much of his life administering large medical institutions, as dean of two prominent medical schools and as president of Sloan-Kettering. He offers both consoling and disturbing reflections. He believes that healthy, vigorous institutions run themselves with a minimum of administrative meddling but that universities should divest themselves of their medical schools and teaching hospitals because of the prospect of enormous financial deficits if the federal government reduces its funding for health research. Medical centers should be publicly funded, Thomas believes, to support the wide range of public services they provide. Without continued funding from NIH, the drain on university endowments to support medical schools and teaching hospitals could be disastrous. It is clear from *The Youngest Science* that Thomas takes great pride in the health benefits brought about by modern medicine and hopes that many of our present medical problems may be solved in the next few decades, although the goal of a completely disease-free human life may take centuries to achieve. Unfortunately, the outbreak of the AIDS epidemic and the appearance of other new infectious diseases have subsequently forced him to revise that overly optimistic prediction.

Late Night Thoughts on Listening to Mahler's Ninth Symphony

In response to the popular success of his first two essay collections, Thomas began working with his editors at Viking Press on a third, which was published in November 1983. In this collection of twenty-four essays, Thomas assembled about half of the essays he had published in *Discover* since 1980, along with miscellaneous pieces from the *New York Review of Books* and the *New England Journal of Medicine. Late Night Thoughts on Listening to Mahler's Ninth Symphony* was received for the most part with polite reviews, although there were some dissenting voices, such as a sharply critical review in *Commentary*.[20]

These essays seem to reflect a continuing trend away from the reflective-meditative mode, toward a shorter, more impersonal, and more deliberative focus on public-policy issues. They demonstrate Thomas's mastery of a concise, flexible, and semicolloquial style that is very effective in focusing on one particular topic or theme. His essay topics range from his enjoyment of the odor of burning leaves in a fall bonfire to the federal government's abandonment of funding for basic research in the sciences in favor of applied weapons research. A tone of somber, pensive apprehension about the threat of nuclear war pervades this collection, giving it a sense of urgency and a note of pessimism lacking in his previous collections.

The twin themes of *Late Night Thoughts* seem to be the helplessness physicians would experience in the face of the overwhelming trauma caused by a thermonuclear exchange and the folly of diverting billions of dollars from basic scientific research to the "Star Wars" applied weapons research—since these weapons would almost certainly never be used. Thomas questions the psychology of nuclear deterrence—the premise of mutually assured annihilation—not as a defense strategist, but as a physician concerned with what could be done for the survivors of a nuclear holocaust. The collection is more topical than either of his two previous books, in response to the apprehensive atmosphere in the early 1980s caused in part by the belligerent rhetoric of Ronald Reagan's first-term administration and by Jonathan Schell's *The Fate of the Earth* (1982), which caused a sensation when it was first serialized in the *New Yorker*.[21] Thomas also supported the work of the Boston-based group Physicians for the Prevention of Nuclear War, which tried to publicize the medical consequences of a thermonuclear exchange. There was also widespread public concern at the time about the global climatic effects of a "nuclear winter," which, according to some scientists, would inevitably follow a massive nuclear exchange, disrupting the earth's biosphere. In fact, three important articles on nuclear winter appeared in *Science* at about the same time that *Late Night Thoughts* was published.[22]

Though Thomas writes as well as ever, this is a less optimistic collection than his first two books. His essays convey the weariness of the humane wisdom of age confronting the hubris of the weapons builders and defense strategists with their elaborate war games. The book's tone is set by the first and last selections, "The Unforgettable Fire" and the title piece, "Late Night Thoughts on Listening to Mahler's Ninth Symphony." The first piece is a long essay-review of *Unforgettable Fire,* a poignant collection of artistic sketches and paintings done by survivors of Hiroshima, and of the seven hundred-page documentary *Hiroshima and Nagasaki: The Physical, Medical, and Social Effects of the Atomic Bombings.*[23] The last piece is a dark and melancholic account of the changes in Thomas's emotional responses to the last movement of Mahler's Ninth Symphony, which used to console him but now fills him with ominous forebodings of the extinction of humanity from thermonuclear war. Recognizing that he was raised in a prenuclear generation, Thomas wonders how young people today cope with the ever-present threat of nuclear war except through denial. "If I were very young, sixteen or seventeen years old," Thomas muses, "I think I would begin, perhaps very slowly and imperceptibly, to go crazy."[24] The essay then concludes with a sardonic account of his watching on television a civil defense official's plausible reassurance of the odds of surviving a nuclear exchange. After hearing such mendacity, Thomas concludes, "I would be twisting and turning to rid myself of human language."[25] The essay ends, appropriately, on the same note of sustained silence as the last movement of Mahler's Ninth Symphony.

Five of the essays in this collection deal in one way or the other with the impact of the nuclear arms race: with the dangers of "thinking the unthinkable" in war strategy; the folly of expecting physicians to treat even a small fraction of the survivors of a nuclear war; the loss of funds from medical research to high-tech weapons research; the dangers of delegating nuclear policy decisions to Pentagon "technicians" obsessed with the power of their weapons and impervious to their consequences; and the psychological impact on the young of the threat of mass destruction. In the face of the collapse of détente and the Reagan administration's repudiation of the SALT II Treaty, Thomas continually stresses the danger of the escalating arms race. Discarding his persona of humane skepticism, Thomas forthrightly condemns administrative policies that have increased world tensions and brought us closer to the threat of nuclear war. Given the atmosphere of gloom in the early 1980s, this essay collection might be considered a humane rationalist's protest against nuclear madness.

The theme of symbiosis is present once again in these essays as a dominant metaphor. In fact, Thomas's perception of the earth as a vast, complex, interrelated organism lends an urgency to his appeals for sanity in arms control and reduction. Another familiar Thomas theme appears in his meditations on the limits of science in attempting to comprehend the vast mystery and inscrutability of life, which modern science has barely begun to penetrate. All scientific research is ultimately worthwhile, he affirms, because it supplies pieces to be fit into the larger puzzle of knowledge that man has slowly assembled. Thomas is a "scientific meliorist" in the sense that Peter Medawar uses the term in his *Advice to a Young Scientist:* Thomas would modestly affirm that the world can be made a better place through the pursuit of learning "acquired and applied to the benefit of all men for the common good."[26] Like Medawar, he would reject the assumption that material prosperity entails spiritual impoverishment—a favorite of those who deride the idea of progress—and would point to the very real gains in human welfare made through advances in medicine and public health, gains now ironically threatened by the misapplication or misuse of advanced weapons technology.[27] Science has become the primary means of advancing our understanding and stewardship of the planet of which we are a crucial part, if indeed our species represents the planet's nascent collective "mind" in the process of emerging. Though there is no certain way to guard against the destructive consequences of technology, we need to do a better job of learning how to anticipate those consequences. "We will need science," he affirms, "to protect us from ourselves."[28]

It is the misuse of technology that worries Thomas most, particularly with the massive budget shift in recent years away from basic research and toward applied science. We are no longer willing to fund the "What if?" proposals, he complains, only the "How to?" Instead of funding basic science projects that will expand our understanding of nature, the $200 billion defense budget is being spent on developing a highly theoretical strategic defense system to protect ourselves against the MIRVs, which are themselves supposed to be developed as a deterrent to war. Thomas insists that this thermonuclear gamesmanship, or brinksmanship—with its speculations about a defensive shield of antimissile missiles, particle beams, and lasar-armed orbiting defense stations, all based on hypothetical technologies—is the most "basic" research and he mordantly claims his citizen's share of the research bonanza. Alluding to Lord Solly Zuckerman's *Nuclear Illusion and Reality,* Thomas argues that the problem is not with basic science but with defense technicians obsessed with the illusion of power, and he forthrightly advocates that the strategic defense initiative, or so-called Star Wars, research be blocked for the good of all mankind.

Some Thoughts on Altruism.   One of Thomas's most controversial essays is his piece entitled "Altruism," in which he examines that puzzling animal behavior in which members of some species sacrifice themselves for the survival of their kin. At first glance it may seem an unnatural act to give away one's life for another, but following the sociobiological argument, Thomas points to the genetic advantages of such behavior. Worker bees may lose their lives when they sting an intruder, or termite soldiers may sacrifice themselves for the sake of the colony, but this makes sense if these social insects are seen as collective organisms. Even the flocking behavior of birds, the herd instincts of zebra or wildebeests, or the schooling behavior of fish may function in this manner. As J. B. S. Haldane has calculated, "I would give up my life for two brothers or eight cousins."[29]

In this and other essays, Thomas shows himself to be strongly influenced by the sociobiological assumption that there is a genetic component to all behavior, even human behavior, though to what degree human behavior is genetically determined is hotly debated. The sociobiologists make the broad analogical leap from the patterned behavior of the social insects to man, but human behavior is so obviously a complex of genetic and cultural factors that we can't even begin to unravel the strands. In a sense, the debate between the sociobiologists and their detractors is the old free-will-versus-determinism argument restated in scientific terms. As Thomas acknowledges, altruistic behavior in humans may have nothing at all to do with genes; there may be no such thing as a gene for self-sacrifice, helpfulness, affection, or even concern, any more than there is a gene for aggression and war. These attributes may be culturally learned or acquired behaviors, but Thomas prefers to believe that there may be a genetic component, a common genome, to keep our species alive and that it may even predispose us to be concerned for other forms of life as well. Perhaps such built-in biological restraints will save us from our own worst follies. Whether this is reductionist reasoning or mere wishful thinking, as some of Thomas's detractors have charged, his essay on altruism offers a biological imperative for the kind of global responsibility that is, in his opinion, our best safeguard against the risk of thermonuclear war.

Elsewhere Thomas has expressed his reservations about strictly reductionist biological explanations of animal behaviors, however. In the essay "Seven Wonders," he returns to an issue of insect behavior that he raised in an earlier uncollected essay, "The Mimosa Girdler." How can it be explained, he asks, that the mimosa girdler has put together three complex pieces of behavior related to egg laying and reproduction? In order to lay its eggs, the insect first has to locate the right tree and climb to the outer limbs; then it has to cut a narrow slit and deposit four or five eggs; and finally it must cut a ring around the live limb so that it will drop to the ground and the eggs will have something to live on once they hatch. The girdling takes several hours and is of no direct benefit to the insect, although the selective pruning thus accomplished does allow the mimosa tree to live longer than it would otherwise. Unpruned, the tree might live about twenty-five years, but with the mimosa girdler's assistance, the tree can live considerably longer. Thomas marvels at how such complex instinctual behavior could arise through natural selection. To our anthropomorphic minds, this set of behaviors has all the characteristics of thinking and planning, but sociobiologists tell us that there are genes selected for this three-step behavior. Thomas is unconvinced. A primitive part of his brain keeps insisting that he's got it all wrong. "That's a smart bug," he muses, "smarter than you'll ever be, and it knows exactly what it is doing every step of the way and why. Trouble is, you don't know how to talk to a girdler, or even listen."[30]

The Memory of Things Past. Though the tone of *Late Night Thoughts* is primarily discursive and impersonal, Thomas does include at least one familiar essay, "The Attic of the Brain," which includes personal anecdotes and allusions. In this meditation on memory, Thomas compares the information we store in our brain cells to the clutter of an old attic, where we stow away old and forgotten possessions for that proverbial rainy day when they might prove to be useful. Rather than clearing out the mental clutter, Thomas favors a certain amount of healthy repression of past experiences, which might be conveniently stored away until, at some later day, they spontaneously pop back into our awareness.

Thomas's title allusion, interestingly, comes from Sir Arthur Conan Doyle's "Study in Scarlet," in which his famous detective, Sherlock Holmes, explains to Watson, "You see, I consider that a man's brain is originally like a little empty attic, and you have to stock it with such furniture as you choose."[31] Doyle himself was a physician—as was his character John Watson—and Doyle set out to create a private detective who would not fail in an assignment because his carefully developed habits of observation and inference form a system of problem solving—a science of deduction. Holmes was fascinated with the little unconscious gestures by which even clever criminals give themselves away. These same kinds of personal idiosyncrasies interest Thomas as manifestations of the self. Consciousness remains a biological mystery, though he is most interested in the mind-brain dualism and what it may reveal about the biological roots of self-awareness. As Thomas points out, the largely autonomous operation and regulation of the body points to the mystery of self-consciousness and to the myth that we are very much in control of ourselves. If the body is capable of such exquisite automatic self-regulation, then what is the purpose of "the ghost in the machine" that we call the self? Is there some driving force in evolution that pushes living forms toward increased self-awareness, both individually and collectively? Thomas is very careful not to express any kind of teleological bias, but he certainly raises the issue of design indirectly through his more visionary speculations, such as his interest in the Gaia hypothesis. Nor does he place himself in the camp of the biological materialists, who would account for the phenomenon of mind strictly in biochemical terms. For Thomas, the scientific returns are not in yet and there are insufficient grounds for any theoretical dogmatism. In fact, he seems to prefer that we remain something of a mystery to ourselves.

Mahler's Ninth Symphony. In the title piece to Thomas's third essay collection, he returns to his interest in classical music, this time not to the baroque world of Johann Sebastian Bach but to the late-nineteenth-century postromanticism of Gustav Mahler. Mahler's Ninth Symphony was his next-to-last orchestral composition, a kind of leave-taking to music and life, a work composed in feverish haste during his 1907 season as conductor of the New York Symphony, with the full knowledge of his illness and probable death. Mahler was morbidly aware that he had a bad heart, that he had little time to work, and that he was killing himself with overwork. Nevertheless, Mahler drove himself to complete this grand orchestral score. Thomas confesses that he used to listen to this symphony with a mixture of melancholy and pleasure, interpreting the music as a reassuring metaphor of the naturalness of death, but that now it fills him with foreboding as his mind swims with images of "a world in which the thermonuclear bombs have begun to explode."[32]

The last movement of Mahler's Ninth Symphony has been widely recognized as the closest musical description of death we have.[33] Mahler himself was intensely well-read, and, perhaps influenced by Nietzsche, he concluded that Western literature and music were dying. His music serves to recapitulate the history of Western music, with its progression from melody to harmony to chromaticism. Melodies pick up and die off but are never fully developed, though there are hints of their resolution. The classical and the romantic strains are blended together and gradually fade into pure chromaticism, with no melodic line, as harmonies are born and die. The first movement of the Ninth Symphony is heavenly, marked by the intense and painful joy of life on earth and a deep premonition of death. In the last movement, Mahler peacefully bids farewell to his own life and to the joys of life on earth. If music is the pulse of life, as Thomas has elsewhere suggested, the dying melodies and pure chromaticism of Mahler's last movement edge toward absolute silence. If, as Thomas describes the process of natural death, "it takes a while for the word to get out to the provinces of the body," then Mahler's Ninth Symphony offers the perfect musical metaphor for the process of dying, as his music always comes back from the edge of silence, as if to say, "I will not die, yet."

Science and Public Policy

In the 1980s, Thomas increasingly took on the role of scientific statesman and spokesman for the scientific establishment on public policy matters. He was invited to give the Elihu Root lectures at the Council on Foreign Relations in New York from 1 to 3 November 1983. This lecture series, entitled "Scientific Frontiers and National Frontiers: A Look Ahead," was later published in *Foreign Affairs*. Thomas's three talks were entitled "Global Interdependence in Science," "Human Health and Foreign Policy," and "Science and the Health of the Earth."[34] His major themes were the need for international scientific cooperation; the responsibility of Western science and technology in alleviating the problems of hunger, disease, and overpopulation in the third world; and the need to develop a global ecological concern for the health of the biosphere. What is most evident in these lectures is Thomas's deep humanity, wisdom, generosity, moral concern, and utter lack of selfish motives. Science fiction writers have popularized the unfortunate stereotype of the scientist as villain, yet the motives ascribed to them—greed, ambition, envy, power—are in fact political motives arising from economic or military rivalry among nation states. They bear little resemblance to the world of science, where teamwork, cooperation, sharing of information, and collaborative research are the norm. Thomas makes the point that science is the one truly international institution where humans are able to put aside political rivalries and cooperate for a common good. It is not limited by national boundaries or ideological preconceptions. Science is not only the best game in town; it is the only game that offers much hope for the future. Unfortunately, in the world of realpolitik, the scientist is an outsider, occasionally consulted but rarely granted access to the corridors of power. He is not so much the decision maker as the scapegoat for the misuse of science and technology to further the ends of power and privilege. Nevertheless, Thomas remains optimistic that given half a chance, the scientific means are available to address the concerns of the next century.

Thomas's faith in science is grounded in the premise of altruism, whether it be culturally or genetically determined. Science, as the most communal of human endeavors (except perhaps for the performing arts), is able to muster a latent will to cooperate, to be helpful, for the benefit of the species and the planet. The global interdependence of science is an immense force capable of acting for the common good, although Thomas is concerned about signs that the freedom of scientific inquiry may be compromised by national rivalries or by private corporate investment in research. Scientific advancement depends on the free exchange of ideas at international conferences and symposia, unhampered by national security concerns or the profit motive. It depends as well on the free movement of research scientists across national borders, so they can collaborate with their colleagues at other laboratories. The biomedical sciences have benefited greatly from this openness in the West, and Thomas hopes that scientific contacts in Eastern Europe can be expanded in the future as well.

The subtitle of Thomas's second Elihu Root lecture, "Human Health and Foreign Policy," could well be "Are Altruism and Cooperation Natural?" since this, after all, is the foreign policy question implicit in any discussion of the obligations that modern, industrialized nations have to the citizens of the underdeveloped nations.[35] Thomas believes that the relatively healthy one-third of the world's population has not only a moral obligation but a deep biological imperative to increase the chances of survival, decent nourishment, and good health for the other two-thirds of the world's population. Thomas believes that our capacity for language ought to bind us together as a social species, though, unfortunately, language differences have more often divided than unified separate cultures. Thomas would like to see the combined resources of the developed world used to alleviate the problems of disease, poverty, and malnutrition, rather than see matters left as they are, with nature taking its course—toward mass famine, ecological disaster, global warfare, or a population crash, the combined effects of which could lead to human extinction. The time is short and much needs to be done, he warns.

What the third world needs is appropriate small-scale public-health assistance; we must correct the immediate problem of contaminated drinking water; we need improvements in agriculture and human nutrition and better methods for treating tropical infectious diseases, especially parasitic diseases. In short, the underdeveloped nations of Africa, Asia, and Latin America need to acquire the same level of basic hygiene achieved in Europe and America before the advent of modern medicine. Our present system of high-cost geriatric health care is not appropriate for nations with a high infant mortality rate that drives a correspondingly high birth rate. Increased funding for expansion of third world public-health and nursing care would go far toward addressing these immediate needs. Thomas envisions something like an expanded World Health Organization, a truly international effort to raise the level of primary health care in the underdeveloped world. Thomas lists the immediate public-health needs as better sanitation, uncontaminated water supplies, antibiotics and vaccines, improved distribution systems for medical supplies, plus a network of small hospitals and local clinics.[36]

Along with improvements in public-health and basic nursing care, Thomas also sees a need for new research in the prevention and treatment of parasitic diseases. The morbidity statistics for tropical parasitic diseases are truly staggering, with perhaps 10 percent of the world's population debilitated or incapacitated by diseases such as malaria, sleeping sickness, and trachoma. The total human-energy costs of amebiasis are difficult to calculate, but it is estimated that a single day of malaria costs the sufferer over five thousand calories.[37] Thomas believes that there are great opportunities for advanced nations to collaborate with third world nations in helping them to develop their own biomedical and biotechnology programs. The reductions in child mortality and the improvements in human health would not necessarily lead to an explosion in the population growth rate, Thomas argues, but might have just the opposite effect, as has been the case in the industrial world.

Thomas's last Elihu Root lecture, "Science and the Health of the Earth," contains his most urgent message concerning the long-term survival of man. He warns that the rate of global deforestation, if not checked, could lead to massive biotic extinctions on a global scale not seen since the late Cretaceous period. Ecologists also predict that massive deforestation could lead to a global "greenhouse effect" from the buildup of carbon dioxide. The survival of our own species is ultimately tied to the health of the biosphere. We will not survive alone. "It is not simply wrong, it is a piece of stupidity on the grandest scale," he warns, "for us to assume that we can simply take over the earth as though it were part farm, part park, part zoo, and domesticate it, and still survive as a species."[38]

Thomas returns to the theme of altruism as offering some hope that we can learn to change our attitudes toward nature and learn to coexist within our ecological niche without upsetting the rest of the earth's ecological balance. Citing evidence from computer simulations using the "prisoner's dilemma" game, Thomas argues that cooperation is the best long-term strategy for staying in the game when there are multiple encounters with other players. Robert Axelrod of the University of Michigan has demonstrated the success of the "tit for tat" cooperative game strategy, devised by Anatol Rapaport, when played against other tactics, such as cheating, aggression, or betrayal.[39] Basically, "tit for tat" assumes that you do what your opponent does: if he cooperates, you do likewise; if he cheats, then you cheat. Cheating may pay off for single encounters, but cooperation wins most of the games in the long run. By analogy, Thomas argues that cooperation offers the best adaptive strategy for long-term survival among multiple species in complex ecosystems. There are, in fact, many examples of coevolution in nature among entirely different species, because of the selective advantage for each. Coevolution and kin selection (or altruistic behavior) are the two primary ways in which species evolve through cooperation rather than competition.

Thomas lists two immediate threats to the world's ecosystem: our incessant energy demands and the threat of thermonuclear war. The increased consumption of fossil fuels threatens to create a greenhouse effect, raising the global temperature and altering the world's climate, and depletion of the ozone layer from nitrogen-oxide pollution means increased exposure to ultraviolet radiation, which could be highly de-structive to the biosphere. But these long-term ecological catastrophes pale in comparison to the immediate risks of all-out nuclear war and the consequent nuclear winter. Thomas deals at length with this issue in an uncollected essay, "TTAPS for the Earth," in which he contends that nuclear war is a no-win proposition for either of the superpowers because of the global devastation involved.[40] There would be no territory gained, no possible winners, no conceivable benefits aside from pure malevolence. Nuclear disarmament has become not merely a diplomatic goal but a moral and biological imperative.

More on Altruism and Coevolution

In the spring of 1984, Thomas was invited to give the Lipkin lectures at the American Museum of Natural History in New York. As the topic for his three lectures, he chose to expand his ideas on the advantages of kin selection and coevolution into something of a personal philosophy.[41] There is some recapitulation from the Root lectures, although Thomas is more explicit here about the subjective nature of his views. His argument is more rhetorical than strictly empirical, based on selective use of the scientific findings of others and anecdotal evidence. Thomas frankly selects his evidence to fit his argument rather than deducing his premises from the full range of available data.

Thomas's basic premise is that cooperation, not competition, is the driving force in nature on a planet with our kind of biosphere. The Darwinian competitive metaphor is only a partial truth; it accounts for obvious cases such as predation but is less useful for understanding how large-scale ecosystems achieve biotic synchrony. Ecologists are far from understanding how complex biotic systems such as tidewater marshes or tropical rain forests function, but coevolution has surely been crucial to their development. The most stable ecosystems are those with the greatest diversity, and that diversity cannot be maintained without a certain degree of cooperation. The noted ecologist Evelyn Hutchinson has pointed out that complex natural communities do not follow the mathematical patterns implicit in the assumption of the "survival of the fittest."[42] Symbiosis is cooperation carried to its extreme, but Thomas argues that "something vaguely resembling symbiosis, less committed and more ephemeral, a sort of *wish* to join up, pervades the biosphere."[43] The evidence he cites ranges from recent work by N. K. Jeon with amoeba nucleus transplants, in which the amoeba nuclei were inadvertently contaminated with a strain of bacteria. The infected amoebas eventually became dependent on the bacteria, which had become symbionts, and were unable to live without them.[44] Thomas interprets this evidence as a kind of biological model illustrating Lynn Margulis's theory of the evolution of eukaryotic cells from more primitive prokaryotic cells. Early in their development, Thomas argues, bacteria learned to live in communities, and there are fossilized stromatolites remarkably similar to living algal mats. These algal communities prospered because they represented more efficient ways of exploiting and recycling essential nutrients. One group, the archaebacteria, which can live in incredibly harsh environments, may well be the oldest living organisms. Some of these bacteria possess DNA strands with "interons," or intervening sequences, similar to ours. The earliest biotic partnerships resulted in the cellular differentiation that made possible the evolution of the photosynthetic cyanobacteria and the respiring aerobic bacteria. The assimilation of chloroplasts into green-plant cells, and mitochondria into all nucleated cells, represents unmistakable progress toward greater complexity, Thomas argues, even though many scientists would reject any imputation of evolutionary design. Bacteria have also worked out chemical signaling mechanisms similar to hormones and peptides. In other words, the basic biochemical mechanisms evolved in advance of the appearance of higher forms of life. Endosymbiosis may indeed be a mechanism by which these higher forms have evolved.

Examples of coevolution abound in nature. Acacia ants protect the acacia tree from other insect predators in return for a place to live. Flowering plants depend upon insects for cross-pollination and have evolved elaborate strategies to attract pollinators, including bright colors, strong odors, and nourishing nectar. Other species of ants "farm" particular varieties of fungus adapted to living in their underground chambers or "tend" aphids for their sweet secretions and use the surplus aphids for food. Kin selection, or altruism, is an extreme form of cooperative behavior among creatures of the same species. The honeybee that eviscerates itself by stinging an intruder is defending the hive. By protecting the hive, the bee is ensuring the preservation of its own genes as well. The long-term odds favor this kind of behavior rather than individual self-preservation. W. D. Hamilton has formulated a mathematical theory of "inclusive fitness" that demonstrates the benefits accruing to the individual from the reproduction of close kin sharing his genes.[45] The overall benefits of cooperation in nature are just as real as those of competition.

The evolution of language is the topic of Thomas's second Lipkin lecture. He argues that humans are distinguished as a social species by their aptitude for language, which is a genetically determined skill. He agrees with Chomsky's theory that there is probably a universal "bio-program" for language development, though it has not yet been discovered. He points to the work that linguist Derek Bickerton has done in studying Hawaiian creole, a language that developed in the nineteenth century, when laborers were imported from China, Korea, Japan, the Philippines, Puerto Rico, and the United States, few of whom could understand the others' speech.[46] A common pidgin language quickly developed, made up of hybrids of words from the various "mother" languages, enabling the laborers to communicate with each other, and the creole eventually evolved from the pidgin. The unique quality of Hawaiian creole is that it formed its own rules of syntax, grammar, and word order, its own articles and prepositions, and its own inflections and indicators of tense and gender. It was in fact a brand-new language.

The evolution of this language, Bickerton asserts, occurred among the first generation of children, particularly those from the age of three up to adolescence, who possess a unique ability for language acquisition. Hawaiian creole was not taught by the parents, and it emerged within the first generation, so it must have developed among children from different language backgrounds who played together. Thomas uses this example from Bickerton's *Roots of Language* to support his assumption of a human genetic predisposition for language that unites us as a social species. He distinguishes among four generic categories of human language: small talk, ordinary language, mathematics, and poetry (or rhymed language), though music should certainly be added here as well. Childhood, he concludes, is essential for humans because it allows time for the language and cultural development that distinguishes us as a species.

Thomas's last Lipkin lecture, entitled "The Puzzlement of Humans," deals with the population crisis, global environmental concerns, and the threat of nuclear war. It is basically a restatement of his Elihu Root lectures, with little that is new. He begins by tracing the growth rate of human population, with its exponential curve, rising toward an inevitable crash if some way is not found to limit population growth voluntarily. He fears that the collective political will may not be there to act effectively and that the alternative controls of starvation, disease, or war will take their toll. Contrasting the decency of individual behavior with the irresponsibility of nations, he fears that Freud may have been right about the existence of an unconscious death wish somewhere in the human mind. Nowhere is this *liebes Tod* more evident than in the perpetuation of the arms race and in our inability to reduce the risks of nuclear war.

Human overpopulation is directly linked to the environmental crisis. We are more concerned with eliminating carcinogens and protecting endangered species than with addressing more serious concerns such as eliminating acid rain, reducing global carbon dioxide emissions, or preventing the pollution of the deep oceans. But these are global concerns, and the international means of controlling them do not exist. Environmental concerns are still a matter of national whim, and for most of the third world, they are perceived as too costly and too great a hindrance to rapid industrial and economic growth. In recent years, UNESCO has proven to be too political to permit the growth of a genuinely collaborative international science, but it still may be our best bet.

The gravest danger of all is the threat of nuclear winter in the aftermath of a nuclear holocaust. Thomas marvels that the TTAPS Report in 1983 did not generate more worldwide interest in preventing a nuclear confrontation, though he feels that the media did not report it adequately. In December 1983, Thomas himself was one of four American scientists invited by Senators Kennedy and Hatfield to testify before a Senate subcommittee panel, along with four Soviet scientists, on the dangers of nuclear winter.[47] The Soviet scientists, experts in climatology and physics, all gave their unqualified support to the TTAPS Report. These findings were echoed in a subsequent scientific paper published in *Nature,* in which three climatologists carried out a more extended three-dimensional computer simulation of the effects of the spreading cloud of dust and radioactive debris after a nuclear exchange.[48] These findings should have made a difference in public opinion and government policy, but they haven't, Thomas concludes, because of ignorance, apathy, or indifference. Or worse, there just may be something too fatally attractive about nuclear weapons and their precise destructive power. We need to buy time to resolve this issue for the most practical of reasons: the preservation of life on the planet. Thomas ends his lecture with a call for cooperative human behavior on a global scale to address the related problems of overpopulation, environmental destruction, and thermonuclear warfare. The best working model for this international cooperation, he concludes, already exists within the scientific community.

Could I Ask You Something?

In the fall of 1984, the library fellows of the Whitney Museum in New York published a 120-copy limited edition of a slim volume of Thomas's poetry and nine original black-and-white etchings by Alfonso Ossorio. Thomas's collaboration with his East Hampton neighbor began a year earlier, when Brendan Gill, who was editing a series for the Whitney Museum, proposed that Thomas and Ossorio work together. The purpose of the series was to bring together the work of distinguished living American authors and artists. Thomas was originally asked to write some brief essays to complement Ossorio's etchings, but he decided that verse would be more appropriate, so he contributed fourteen poems. Neither Thomas nor Ossorio felt that they were illustrating or glossing the work of the other; instead, the work was, in Thomas's words, a genuine collaboration. According to Thomas: "We combined Surrealism and biology. There is a lot of Surrealism in biology a lot of the time, anyway."[49]

Writing the poems for *Could I Ask You Something?* allowed Thomas to return to his early interest in poetry. Many of the fourteen poems in this volume reflect Thomas's usual preoccupations: symbiosis, synchrony, and the unity of all life on earth.[50] All are written in free verse, two as prose poems or short, lyrical essays and the others as lyrical meditations of various lengths. Many of his poems employ a first-person persona, but the focus is still less on the narrator's moods or feelings than on the biological theme or idea developed. Like the late poems of Loren Eiseley, these lyrical meditations are derived from Thomas's earlier prose writings. They demonstrate that good scientific poetry is difficult to compose without becoming too discursive. These are for the most part discursive poems, short, lyrical correlatives to his essays. None is really distinctive, even as nature poetry. Thomas's poems lack the intellectual rigor, tension, and intensity of A. R. Ammons's biological verse. There is no conflict or drama in Thomas's verse, no narrative, none of the striking originality of voice that creates memorable poetry. Poetry cannot bear too great a weight of exposition without a lyrical counterpoint. Otherwise the verse lines do not chant or sing but remain prosaic and simply enunciate. Thomas has recognized his poetic limitations and has spoken elsewhere of his "good bad verse," perhaps as a way of disarming critics, although there he was referring to his medical school limericks and doggerel that he reprinted in the appendix to *The Youngest Science,* poetry clearly written in a lighter voice than his late poems.[51] Somehow the light occasional verse of his medical school days, with its bantering tone and easy witticisms, better fits the Thomas persona than does the meditative, philosophical voice of his late poems, which seems more appropriate to the essay than to poetry. Or perhaps it is just that few scientists are accomplished poets as well.

For instance, his title selection, "Could I Ask You Something?" a four-paragraph prose poem, recapitulates Thomas's notion of his body as a composite organism, a symbiotic assemblage of molecules and cells. The body as an ecosystem is an intriguing metaphor, but it seems better developed in *The Lives of a Cell* than here. A more interesting poem is "Night Song," a four-stanza mystical account of an experience of cosmic inclusiveness. In each stanza, the refrain introduces a different persona lodging within the self: judge, guest, friend, and heart. "Night Song" is a poem about the mystical experience of holding the cosmos in the palm of one's hand: the moon the size of a coin, a century shrunk to a shout, a terrestrial embryo, and the universe shrunk to a number embedded in amber. Thomas's imagery recalls that of Julian of Norwich, a fourteenth-century medieval nun and mystic who wrote in her *Revelations:* "And he showed me a little thing the size of a hazelnut in the palm of my hand, and it was round as a ball. I looked thereupon with the eye of my understanding and thought: What may this be? And it was answered generally thus: it is all that is made."[52]

An admirer of her work, Thomas comments that these simple lines ring with ambiguity and are profound enough to speak to modern cosmological physicists. Thomas's "Night Song" echoes his essay meditations on the cell as a community, on the structural complexities contained in the smallest forms of life.

"New Birds" is a meditation on the mysteries of evolution and extinction. If the birds do not sing here any more, perhaps they can be conjured back from the reptilian genes that may hold within them the mysteries of flight and bird song. "There Is Another God" contrasts a mechanistic deism with the personal reassurance of a local God of place and habitat, a God of green valleys and warm stones rather than distant nebulas. "Washington Square Nature Note" contrasts the comfortable security of being earthbound with the reverie of tacking on a solar wind and exploring the cosmos. "Keep Your Head Down" reminds us, as Thomas has facetiously remarked, that "nature abounds with little round things."[53] Fleas, roaches, germs, lichens—all are pieces of the great thought of nature. "Earth-Orbital" recalls Thomas's visionary sense of the earth as Gaia, a unified organism reaching toward self-consciousness through orbiting satellites that monitor the health of the biosphere. "Nature-Note: The Empire State Building" comments on the lack of pine trees or lichens growing on the exterior structure: it has not yet been colonized by the forces of nature.

"We Live Inside Each Other" is a six-stanza lyric meditation that celebrates Thomas's theme of the ecological unity of the biosphere, in which living matter is continually recycled from one organism to another. We are literally a part of each other's cytoplasm as we exchange molecules. Thomas's sense of the mystical unity of life becomes more explicit in this poem, as he articulates the shimmering vision of life's synchrony inherent in his essays. Rich in biotic imagery, the lines envision plankton, birds, children, maple leaves, cicadas, gnats, and gannets all swimming the same tides of life. The perspective shifts in "Jet-Borne" to twelve miles in the sky, as the narrator looks down and imagines the myriad pulsating exchanges of energy of life occurring below him. In the next poem, "Earth Tide," Thomas imagines the impact of the moon's gravitational force on the earth's ecosystem, as leaves, roots, insects, and plankton all respond to the rise and fall of the planetary tides. "Prediction" imagines what the great terrestrial thought will be once we are all linked together in global consciousness: a desire to extend ourselves outward like mold spores, colonize the planets, and tack our sheets to a solar wind as the earth projects its first cosmic thought. The last piece, "And Did You Know," is another prose poem that echoes the tone and mood of the opening piece. Here Thomas personifies the major components of the cell—ribosomes, mitochondria, centrioles, cilia, and nucleus—in a deft and clever heuristic piece that illustrates by metaphor and analogy how these organelles function within the cell. It would make a wonderful illustrated introduction to the cell for young biology students.

Perhaps the most successful Thomas poem is "On Insects," which describes the instinctual world of the social insects. Inside the labyrinthine walls of the colony, ants jerkily communicate by touch, while bees dance the route to Sunday morning's asters. Most of what transpires, however, with both insects and humans, is small talk. Through this ritual contact, Thomas implies, we affirm ourselves and live anew. Touch and live again. What comes through most of all in these poems is Thomas's unbounded aesthetic appreciation of the beauty and vitality of life, which he has been privileged to glimpse through a lifetime of biomedical research.

Chapter Five
The Medical Humanist: Thomas as a Model

As a writer, Lewis Thomas has demonstrated a remarkable mastery of the short-essay form, a flexible genre that he has shaped and molded to his own purposes. He has used the openness of the essay form to cultivate a distinct persona as physician, teacher, and poet, speaking through his essays with wit, irony, and humor on a wide range of medical and scientific topics. Reading Thomas is an education, not only in how to enjoy and appreciate science as an intellectual endeavor but in how to think clearly, lucidly, and undogmatically about major policy issues involving science and the public interest. The remarkable popularity of his essays demonstrates that they address a deep public need to learn more about science and to have new research discoveries presented clearly and objectively, without undue technicality or condescension.

Largely through Thomas's success, medical narrative, essays, and reportage have taken an increasingly important place in contemporary American nonfiction prose. Though a few predecessors such as Paul De Kruif's *Microbe Hunters* (1926), Hans Zinsser's *Rats, Lice, and History* (1937), and Berton de Rouche's *Eleven Blue Men* (1953) had been able to find a popular market for narratives of medical history or detection, it remained for Thomas to define a popular audience for the biomedical essay recast as personal reflection on a wide variety of scientific and social issues. Whether through the attractiveness of the Thomas persona, or through his mythopoetic vision of global community based on symbiosis and cooperation, Thomas has demonstrated that it is possible to write about complex medical issues for a general audience, and not just for other professionals. His success with the familiar essay as a medium for scientific reflection has made it possible for a number of other fine contemporary biomedical writers, such as Oliver Sacks, Richard Selzer, Gerald Weissman, Harold J. Morowitz, and Milton J. Slocum, to find an audience for their work.[1] And in a broader sense, Thomas, along with Loren Eiseley, Stephen Jay Gould, and others, has helped to popularize the science essay as a respectable nonfiction prose form and to broaden the audience for good science writing.

Thomas's unique mastery of the short-essay form is marked by a distinctive vision of organic harmony, articulated in a reassuring, colloquial style that communicates complex scientific ideas without losing the readers. His success stems from the medical authority of the Thomas persona, combined with modesty, sometimes ironic but more often genuine, in the face of the vast mysteries of nature and the honest recognition of how much we still do not understand about the world. In an age of widespread medical overspecialization, Thomas has managed to convey through his essays the clarity and directness of the old-fashioned family practitioner. Though he often deals with complex and difficult issues, he never lapses into the obscurity of highly detailed technical discourse. Yet he still conveys a genuine respect for ideas and a sense of the enormous intellectual attraction of science. There is more honest doubt and wonder than dogmatism and authority in his manner. Thomas recognizes that we live in times of doubt and uncertainty, when people question the authority of science and are anxious about the complexity of issues that seem dangerous but beyond their comprehension. Much of what Thomas conveys is reassurance, and perhaps this accounts for much of his appeal.

Thomas also offers a model of lucid prose writing and deft rhetorical skill, which have made his essays popular in virtually every freshman English anthology. *The Lives of a Cell* has also been used in numerous introductory biology courses, as a means of interesting nonscience majors in the living world. Thomas has been justly critical of many of the methods of teaching undergraduate science courses, and of the rigidity of the premedical curriculum, and he offers fresh thoughts on how science courses can be made more attractive. It is vitally important that we do a better job of teaching mathematics and the physical and natural sciences on the secondary and undergraduate levels. This task challenges scientists to become better communicators. The scientific community must also recognize the values implicit in their work and accept the fact that like it or not, science conveys a distinct philosophy of life.

Thomas, like his British contemporary Sir Peter Medawar, is an accomplished science writer who articulates a coherent philosophy of nature. Both Thomas and Medawar recognize the role of the scientist's vision, of the premises and preconceptions that shape scientific research and help to determine which problems will be pursued. Both are frank in recognizing the motives and limitations of science, the importance of collaboration, and the qualities of good research. Both acknowledge the culture of science and recognize how important it is to convey, through well-written scientific memoirs, how scientists actually live and work. Both are passionately committed to the ethics of science: to the cultivation of an open, critical mind, the maintenance of empirical skepticism and rigor, and the disinterested pursuit of truth. Most of all, despite the uncertainties of this century, both share a deep and abiding optimism about human prospects for the future, based on their faith in the resiliency of the human mind and spirit. An excerpt from Medawar's essay "The Effecting of All Things Possible," which was read by Lady Jean Medawar at his memorial service, well expresses this shared outlook.

We cannot point to a single definitive solution of any one of the problems that confronts us—political, economic, social, or moral, that is, having to do with the conduct of life. We are still beginners, and for that reason may hope to improve. To deride the hope of progress is the ultimate fatuity, the last word in poverty of spirit and meanness of mind. There is no need to be dismayed by the fact that we cannot yet envisage a definitive solution of our problems, a resting-place beyond which we need not try to go.[2]

If, as Georg Lukács has argued, the essay represents the purest form of abstract discourse, in which ideas themselves are the most prominent element, and provides the purest and most transparent reflection of the author's mind and sensibility, then Thomas must be credited with bringing these same qualities to the modern science essay.[3] Thomas has used the essay to raise important philosophical questions in modern science and medicine. If the essence of the short familiar essay is focus, then through Thomas's essays one enjoys the unique experience of viewing the world of scientific ideas through the microscope of the author's imagination, and of examining that world in close detail.

Thomas has been so successful at everything to which he has applied himself—medicine, biomedical research, administration—that his career as an essayist seems almost an afterthought. Yet the comparisons of his essays to those of Montaigne are not entirely hyperbole. In their tone of frank, honest good humor, skeptical interest, and abiding faith in human nature, the style of Thomas's essays and the persona that lies behind them bear much in common with the great sixteenth-century French writer who has been called the father of the modern essay. If Thomas is finally something of a mystic, his mystical inclinations grow out of his aesthetic delight and reverence for the intricate and beautiful design of the natural world and for the endlessly fascinating mechanisms of life. His is an informed mysticism, held in check by his skepticism and his scientific rationalism but nurtured by his humane learning and his fascination with all aspects of human nature, especially language and music, those cultural expressions that make us most human.

Appendix:
An Interview with Lewis Thomas

The following interview with Dr. Lewis Thomas took place on 2 August 1984, in his office at the Sloan-Kettering Memorial Center in Manhattan. I came with a prearranged set of questions, but what actually followed was a wide-ranging and unrehearsed discussion of his career and interests. On the sixth floor of Sloan-Kettering, I stepped off the elevator and entered a long hallway cluttered with research apparatus that seemed to spill out of the labs. After some difficulty, I found Dr. Thomas's office, where his secretary asked me to wait until he arrived. I was looking over my notes when Dr. Thomas appeared, tall and distinguished, bespectacled, wearing an open white lab coat, shirt, and tie. I was immediately impressed with his keen, penetrating glance and his relaxed demeanor. He invited me into his office and apologized for the boxes and clutter, explaining that he had recently retired as an active officer at Sloan-Kettering and was packing his books and papers to send to his home in East Hampton, Long Island. He mentioned that he had just accepted a position as visiting professor at the State University of New York, Stony Brook, where he would be working with faculty in English, biology, and medicine. At that point I began to ask him some questions.

Q: Dr. Thomas, given the enthusiastic reception of your first four books, do you have any plans for further publication?

A: All but one of the essays in the *New England Journal of Medicine* have been published. Since 1976, I have quit writing for the *New England Journal of Medicine,* but I have written on and off for *Discover* magazine.

Q: Have some of your essays been revised or collected under different titles than those under which they were initially published? I believe that your essays continued to appear in the *New England Journal of Medicine* until March 1980. Did you leave additional essays with the editor, Dr. Franz Ingelfinger?

A: That's right.

Q: Do you have any plans for forthcoming books?

A: There will be a collection of essays and poems forthcoming in November [1984] from the Whitney Museum in a private printing of 150 copies, edited by Brendan Gill. It will include fourteen new poems, the three Elihu Root lectures in foreign affairs, and the three Museum of Natural History lectures in the Matt Lipkin Lecture Series, "Man's Place in Nature." The book will also include nine original etchings by the East Hampton artist Alfonso Ossorio.

Q: How did your interest in writing develop?

A: When I was an undergraduate at Princeton, I had some interest in poetry and read Pound and Eliot. It was not until I was a senior that I became interested in biology. While I was an intern in Boston I wrote some poems that were published in the *Atlantic Monthly*. I wrote late at night in the Peabody Building [of Boston City Hospital] and left a folder there accidentally. A Scottish friend found the folder and sent the poems off to a literary agent in New York, Russell & Walker [A. E. Russell's son]. The agent liked the poems and I was paid thirty-five dollars a poem when they were published in the *Atlantic,* which was good money in those days. Later at Johns Hopkins, I published some poems in the *Hopkins Literary Review*. I met William Carlos Williams once when he made a house call because some relative had him as a pediatrician.

Q: What about the essay form in particular?

A: Though I always liked reading essays, and Montaigne in particular, I began writing essays on invitation for a 1970 conference on inflammation in Kalamazoo, Michigan. I gave the keynote address there, and it was later reprinted and sent to the conference participants. My old friend, Franz Ingelfinger, who was then editing the *New England Journal of Medicine,* saw the reprint and asked whether I would consider writing a monthly column for him. I was only allowed one page— about 1100 words—of space. I can't follow an outline—my writing depends on spontaneity. I tried writing some essays according to an outline and found them too stiff and formal, so with a *Journal* deadline approaching, I simply sat down and wrote until I finished what I had to say. And then I mailed them off to Ingelfinger. Writing poems and essays is great fun—it's something of a surprise. It offers the same combination of freedom and surprise as doing research. Part of the pleasure is in telling someone about it. An example of this kind of science writing that comes to mind is Erwin Chargaff's *Heraclitean Fire.* Writing scientific papers is different. I find the flat, third-person, passive style uncongenial.

Q: What about your essay topics? Were they originally assigned by your editor, or were you free to write about whatever you chose?

A: The choice was my own. The topics came from scientific papers I had read, but the style and approach were my own.

Q: You entitled your memoir *The Youngest Science: Notes of a Medicine-Watcher,* but isn't medicine as much of an art as a science?

A: Medicine will become a *real* science as we learn more about the mechanisms of human disease. Some day we will be able to prevent or reverse most serious diseases. Absolutely impenetrable problems are beginning to yield new answers. There are no questions of cells or tissues that can't be gotten at. With DNA, for example, and genetics, the roof is about to fall in for biology and physics. We are getting at the underlying mechanics. There are total surprises in store, good leads, and great fun. In scientific research today, it is much harder to master more than one discipline because of the high degree of specialization. Great masses of highly reductionistic data are being collected.

What are the fundamental scientific disciplines? It's much harder to tell them apart because of the similar fundamental mechanisms involved. In immunology, many new discoveries are now being made, but there are still many unanswered questions. How do sets of cells communicate with each other? What are the networks of cellular reactants? There are other sets of new problems for the embryologists. We will see new hybrid disciplines, such as neurobiology.

Q: You have been involved in so many fields of medical research. What was your own training like?

A: After my internship, I spent two years residency in neurology and then the war came along. Dr. Thomas Rivers, the head of the Rockefeller University Naval Medical Research Unit, asked me to join. We studied scrub fever, typhus, virology, and bacteriology. After the war, I went to Johns Hopkins, where I studied rheumatic fever; at Tulane I studied infectious disease; at Minnesota, I enjoyed a *settee* in medicine and pediatrics; at Bellevue, I was a clinician; and later I was dean at NYU. During the 1950s, with NIH, there were exhilarating times, but research hopes may have been raised too high. And now funds for basic research are being cut back.

Q: If we could change the topic, and discuss your career as an author for a moment, were you surprised at the success of your first book, *The Lives of a Cell?*

A: Yes, I was surprised at the popular reception of my essays, and the publisher [Viking Press] was astonished. Now Oxford University Press is interested in picking up all of the books, which will be republished as the collected essays. My books have now been translated into twelve languages. I translated them myself for the French and German editions. The translator of the Czech edition made me out to be a materialist, a Marxist-Leninist.

Q: Whom do you hope to reach with your essays? What audience interests you the most?

A: The college and student readership pleases me the most. Recently I met with some students from my high school alma mater, the McBurney School in Manhattan. I've just retired from a university professorship at SUNY–Stony Brook, where I chaired a committee on the life sciences and medicine. I was a real "academic tramp"—I worked with faculty in the natural sciences, English, and the medical school. I believe the influence of premedical education is malign. The premed students are a cheerless bunch—hotly competitive, but no fun at all to teach.

Q: To change the topic again, you described your childhood in some detail in *The Youngest Science.* Have you been back to your home in Flushing at all?

A: I drove through recently on Northern Boulevard, and the only landmark is the Long Island Railroad tracks. All of the old neighborhood is gone, replaced by apartments. The Dutch Reformed Church we attended is now a Korean Protestant Church. There has been a huge influx of new immigrants. I attended Flushing High School for one year, but my parents felt that it was too crowded. There were more than twenty students per class. So I commuted in to Manhattan on the Long Island Railroad and attended the McBurney School. My interest in medicine was stimulated by my father, a highly respected general practitioner who later became a surgeon at Flushing Memorial Hospital.

At this point, we had been talking for about an hour, and Dr. Thomas had to excuse himself because he had another appointment. I did not have an opportunity to ask him any of the remaining questions, and problems with scheduling did not permit us to arrange a follow-up interview.

Notes and References

Chapter One

1. Jeremy Bernstein, "Lewis Thomas: Life of a Biology Watcher," *Experiencing Science* (New York: Basic Books, 1978), 169–70.
2. *The Youngest Science* (New York: Viking Press, 1983), 23.
3. Ibid., p. 253. Princeton University Alumni Records give the date as 1 November 1906, however.
4. *Youngest Science,* 3. All other quotes in this paragraph are from p. 23.
5. As related in an interview with Nicholas Falco, head, Long Island Division, Queensborough Public Library, Jamaica, New York, on 26 December 1984. See also "New P.S. 20 Named after John Bowne," *Long Island Star Journal,* 29 October 1948, 2; and "Daniel Carter Beard," in *Famous Men of Flushing* (Flushing: Flushing Historical Society, 1943).
6. *Youngest Science,* 1–2.
7. Interview with Mrs. Richard Brown, 27 June 1985.
8. *Youngest Science,* 9–10.
9. Interview with Mrs. Richard Brown, 27 June 1985.
10. *Youngest Science,* 18.
11. Ibid., 24.
12. Ibid., 228.
13. This anecdote is mentioned by Bradford D. Jones, letter to the author, 29 May 1985.
14. Flushing High School records. As conveyed in 12 March 1985 letter from school historian, Joel Fleishman, to the author.
15. *McBurneian,* Senior Issue, 1929, 13. The various clubs were identified in a 27 June 1985 letter from director of development, Mary Ellen Goodman, to the author.
16. *McBurneian,* 15.
17. Ibid., 29.
18. *Youngest Science,* 26.
19. 12 June 1985 letter from Arthur S. Hudson to the author.
20. 15 July 1985 letter from Arthur S. Hudson to the author.
21. Woodrow Wilson made these remarks in his address to the Chicago alumni on 28 November 1902. See *The Papers of Woodrow Wilson,* vol. 14, ed. Arthur S. Link (Princeton: Princeton University Press, 1972), 223. Regarding the preceptorial system, see Alexander Leitch, *A Princeton Companion* (Princeton: Princeton University Press, 1978), 374–75.

22. For further discussion of Wilson's educational reforms, see Hardin Craig, *Woodrow Wilson at Princeton* (Norman: University of Oklahoma Press, 1960); and Charles Grosvenor Osgood, "Woodrow Wilson," in *The Lives of Eighteen from Princeton,* ed. Willard Thorp (Princeton: Princeton University Press, 1946), 282–301.

23. This freshman anecdote is contained in a 6 June 1985 letter from Bradford D. Jones to the author.

24. *Youngest Science,* 26.

25. Ibid., 26–27.

26. *Princeton Tiger,* 21 October 1932, 17. "Reflections on the Investigation" appeared in the 28 April 1932 issue of the *Tiger,* p. 15; and "Reflections on the Evil of Drink" in the 19 May 1932 issue, p. 12. All were signed "L.T." Mr. Earle E. Coleman, Princeton University archivist, was kind enough to identify these poems and send me copies.

27. "Princeton's Movie Industry" appears in the 18 February 1931 issue of the *Tiger,* p. 23, along with "Something New in Advertising," p. 21. "Like a Light" appears in the 3 June 1931 issue, p. 25, and "The Huddle" in the 21 October 1931 issue, p. 22. All of these pieces are signed "ELTIE."

28. "The Horror at Fuhrtbang" appears in the 25 November 1931 issue of the *Tiger,* p. 23, signed "ELTIE." "Christmas Comes to the Jukes Family" was printed in the 14 December 1932 issue, p. 16, signed "L.T."

29. These comments appear in a Princeton University faculty memorial resolution for Wilbur Willis Swingle, dated 3 November 1975. Princeton University Archives.

30. *Youngest Science,* 27.

31. Ibid.

32. Ibid., 28.

33. James Bordley III, M.D., and A. McGehee Harvey, M.D., *Two Centuries of American Medicine, 1776–1976* (Philadelphia: W. B. Saunders, 1976), 157.

34. Harvey Cushing, *The Life of Sir William Osler,* (Oxford: Clarendon Press, 1925), 1:552.

35. Emile Holman, M.D., "Osler and Halsted, a Contrast in Personalities," in *Humanism in Medicine,* ed. John P. McGovern, M.D., and Chester R. Burns, M.D., (Springfield, Ill.: Charles C. Thomas, 1973), 23.

36. "Future Prospects for Basic Science in Medicine," *Bulletin of the American Academy of Arts and Sciences* 34, 1 (October 1980): 23.

37. Ibid., 24.

38. H. Sherwood Lawrence, "Presentation of The George M. Kober Medal to Lewis Thomas," *Transactions of the Association of American Physicians* 96 (1983): cxix.

39. See "Hermann Blumgart, M.D.," *New England Journal of Medicine* 296 (12 May 1977): 1117–18; and "Hermann Blumgart: An Appreciation,"

Circulation 33 (January 1966): 4–5. See also 11 July 1985 interview with Dr. Eugene Stead.

40. *Youngest Science,* 32. See also Henry K. Beecher and Mark D. Altschule, *Medicine at Harvard: The First Three Hundred Years* (Hanover, N.H.: University Press of New England, 1977).

41. *Youngest Science,* 5, 249–53. Two more examples of his medical school verse are "Ode to Maloof" and "Lines Dedicated to Leo Alexander," Ibid., 258–60.

42. Francis W. Peabody, M.D., *Doctor and Patient* (New York: Macmillan, 1930), 31.

43. *Youngest Science,* 37.

44. Interview with Dr. Eugene Stead, 11 July 1985.

45. *Youngest Science,* 29.

46. Ibid., 241.

47. See "Franz Ingelfinger, M.D.: A Redoubtable Character," *Journal of the American Medical Association* 243 (1 February 1980): 409–414; "Franz Ingelfinger, Editor Emeritus," *New England Journal of Medicine* 296 (23 June 1977): 1475–76; and "Franz Ingelfinger, 1910–1980," *New England Journal of Medicine* 302 (10 April 1980): 859–60.

48. *Youngest Science,* 242.

49. As recalled by Dr. Franz J. Ingelfinger in *The Harvard Medical Unit at Boston City Hospital,* vol. 2, pt. 1, "The Peabody-Minot Tradition, 1915–1950," compiled by Maxwell Finland and William B. Castle (Boston: Harvard Medical School, 1983), 315.

50. As recalled by Thomas, Ibid., 336–37.

51. *Youngest Science,* 256–57. Of these poems, I have only been able to find seven in print. See Bibliography.

52. Ibid., 256–57.

53. *Atlantic Monthly* 167 (March 1941): 372.

54. Ibid. (May 1941): 636.

55. Ibid. (April 1941): 502.

56. *Harper's Bazaar* 75 (October 1941): 138.

57. *Atlantic Monthly* 168 (December 1941): 738.

58. *Youngest Science,* 74. In Thomas's professional bibliography, his first scientific paper is dated 1943, however.

59. Ibid., 72–73.

60. Ibid., 74.

Chapter Two

1. Lawrence, "Kober Medal," cxxi. See also "Peabody-Minot Tradition," 412.

2. Ibid. See also *Youngest Science,* 75.

3. These findings were published as L. Thomas and J.H. Dingle, "Investigations of Meningococcal Infection: Bacteriological Aspects," *Journal of Clinical Investigations* 22 (1943): 353–59.

4. *Youngest Science,* 75–77.

5. Ibid., 78.

6. Ibid., 77–78.

7. Ibid., 92.

8. Ibid., 93.

9. Bernstein, "Lewis Thomas," 182.

10. "Limitation," *Atlantic Monthly* 174 (October 1944): 119.

11. "Three Poems: Ward Rounds, Meditation—103 Fahrenheit, and Plant a Metal Seed," *Hopkins Review* 1, no. 2 (Spring 1948): 38–41.

12. "On Insects," *New Yorker* 47 (10 July 1971): 28.

13. All quotations from Philip Y. Paterson, "LT/EAE and the MS Quest: Going to the Dogs and Rats to Study the Patient," *Cellular Immunology* 82, no. 1 (November 1983): 58.

14. Ibid., 71.

15. *Youngest Science,* 108–109.

16. The proceedings from this conference were later published by the Minnesota Heart Association in *Rheumatic Fever: A Symposium Held at the University of Minnesota on November 29, 30, and December 1, 1951,* ed. Lewis Thomas (Minneapolis: University of Minnesota Press, 1952).

17. Lewis W. Wannamaker, "The Pathogenesis of Rheumatic Fever: Lewis Thomas and the Minnesota Years," *Cellular Immunology* 82, no. 1 (November 1983): 82–83.

18. As quoted in Wannamaker, Ibid., 82.

19. Interview with Dr. Floyd W. Denny, M.D., Chapel Hill, 14 July 1986, and 11 September 1986 letter from Dr. Denny.

20. *Youngest Science,* 163–65.

21. Ibid., 113.

22. Cited in Eden Graber, "Immunology at NYU, 1955–1968/The Seminal Years," *NYU Physician* 39, no. 1 (Fall 1982): 7.

23. Graber, "Immunology," 6.

24. Cited in Graber, "Immunology," 6.

25. Graber, "Immunology," 4.

26. Cited in Graber, "Immunology," 7.

27. Graber, "Immunology," 10.

28. Cited in Graber, "Immunology," 13.

29. Lawrence, "Kober Medal," cxxvii.

30. Ibid.

31. "A Possible Mechanism for the Action of Cortisone in Reactions to Tissue Injury," in *International Symposium on Injury, Inflammation, and Immunity,* ed. Lewis Thomas, M.D., Jonathan W. Uhr, M.D., and Lester Grant, M.D. (Baltimore: Williams and Wilkins Company, 1964), 312–17.

32. From the transcript of a speech by Dr. Saul J. Farber, M.D., at City Council President Stein's Health Care Hearing, 22 July 1986.

33. Cited in Frank W. Lopez, "The Bellevue Connection," *NYU Physician* 39, no. 3 (Spring 1983): 4.

34. *Youngest Science,* 130–33.

35. Cited in Lopez, "Bellevue Connection," 11.

36. *Youngest Science,* 134.

37. "Heroin," *New England Journal of Medicine* 286 (9 March 1972): 531–33. Though the article contains some interesting public-policy proposals, Thomas did not include it in *The Lives of a Cell,* either because it did not fit the overall theme of the essay collection or perhaps because he felt it was too controversial to be reprinted.

38. *Youngest Science,* 144–45.

39. "A Note to the Class of 1967 from the Dean," *Medical Violet* (1967), 7.

40. As noted in an interview with Dr. Gregory Siskind, Cornell University Medical Center, New York, on 24 July 1986.

41. Interview with Mr. Albert Fuller in New York City, 25 July 1986.

42. As noted in an interview with Dr. Martin S. Begun, associate dean, NYU Medical School, 23 July 1986.

43. *Youngest Science,* 181–82.

44. As noted in an interview with Dr. Wallace Clyde, UNC–Chapel Hill School of Medicine, 8 July 1986.

45. Ibid.

46. Cited in Marjorie Blake Noyes, "The New Dean," *Yale Medicine* 7, no. 2 (Spring 1972): 17.

47. "A Century of Commitment: A History of Memorial Sloan-Kettering Cancer Center" (New York: Archives Committee of Memorial Sloan-Kettering Cancer Center, 1984), 16.

48. Thomas discusses these findings in chap. 19 of *The Youngest Science,* "Olfaction and the Tracking Mouse," 208–219. See also Gary K. Beauchamp, Kunio Yamazaki, and Edward A. Boyse, "The Chemosensory Recognition of Genetic Individuality," *Scientific American* 253, no. 1 (July 1985): 86–92.

49. Beauchamp et al., "Chemosensory Recognition," 86.

50. Ibid., 92.

51. As noted in an interview with Dr. Saul J. Farber, dean of NYU Medical School, 23 July 1986.

52. "Peabody-Minot Tradition," 338.

53. Saul J. Farber, "A Tribute to Lewis Thomas," *Cellular Immunology* 82, no. 1 (November 1983): 21.

Chapter Three

1. In chap. 22 of *The Youngest Science,* Thomas recounts how he began writing essays in midcareer. See especially pp. 239–44.

2. Ibid., 243–44.

3. See Bibliography for exact citations.

4. Besides "Heroin," these two uncollected essays are "The Mimosa Girdler," *New England Journal of Medicine* 301 (29 November 1979): 1224–26; and "On Science Business," *New England Journal of Medicine* 302 (17 January 1980): 157–58.

5. "Ceti," in *The Lives of a Cell* (New York: Viking Press, 1974), 43.

6. "An Earnest Proposal," in *Lives of a Cell,* 29.

7. "Adaptive Aspects of Inflammation" was originally presented as the keynote address at the Third Symposium of the International Inflammation Club at Brook Lodge, Michigan, held from 1 to 3 June 1970. It was later reprinted in *Immunopathology of Inflammation,* ed. Bernard K. Forscher and John C. Houck, Excerpta Medica Congress Series *no. 229* (Amsterdam: Excerpta Medica, 1971), 1–10.

8. Ibid., 2.

9. Ibid., 3.

10. Ibid.

11. Lynn Margulis's *Origin of Eukaryotic Cells* (New Haven: Yale University Press, 1970) appeared about a year before Thomas began writing his monthly columns for the *New England Journal of Medicine,* and his first six essays show the strong influence of her book, an influence he acknowledges. Thomas's perspective here seems to be much influenced by her innovative theories of evolution by endosymbiosis. See especially Lynn Margulis, "Symbiosis and Evolution," *Scientific American* 225, no. 2 (August 1971): 48–57. She later revised and expanded her theories in *Symbiosis in Cell Evolution: Life and Its Environment on the Early Earth* (New York: W. H. Freeman, 1981).

12. "Adaptive Aspects," 3.

13. "Some Biomythology," in *Lives of a Cell,* 126.

14. "Sensuous Symbionts of the Sea," *Natural History* 80, no. 4 (August–September 1971): 37. Though this essay has never been collected, it anticipates many of the themes in his two later books.

15. Ibid., 28.

16. Although Lovelock and Margulis published their paper in 1974, Thomas may have seen their paper in manuscript form at an earlier date. See James E. Lovelock and Lynn Margulis, "Atmospheric Homeostasis by and for the Atmosphere," *Tellus* 26 (1974): 1–9.

17. J. E. Lovelock, *Gaia: A New Look at Life on Earth* (New York: Oxford University Press, 1979), ix.

18. "Vibes," in *Lives of a Cell,* 41.

19. Foreword to Miroslav Holub, *Sagittal Section: Poems New and Selected,* trans. Stuart Friebert and Dana Habova, Field Translation Series no. 3. (Oberlin: Oberlin College, 1980), [1].

20. George Lakoff and Mark Johnson, *Metaphors We Live By* (Chicago: University of Chicago Press, 1980), 5. See also chap. 6, "Science as Metaphor," in K. C. Cole, *Sympathetic Vibrations: Reflections on Physics as a Way of Life* (New York: William Morrow & Co., 1985), 155–78.

21. Cited in J. Silberner, "Metaphor in Immunology," *Science News* 130 (16 October 1980): 254.

22. "Germs," in *Lives of a Cell*, 76.

23. "Your Very Good Health," in *Lives of a Cell*, 82.

24. Ibid., 85.

25. Ibid., 56. The quote comes from chap. 5 of Browne's seventeenth-century discourse on burial customs. See Sir Thomas Browne, *Religio Medici and Other Works* (Oxford: Clarendon Press, 1964), 119.

26. "Death in the Open," in *Lives of a Cell*, 99.

27. "The Long Habit," in *Lives of a Cell*, 50. In this essay, Thomas is also clearly responding to the lively debate in the early 1970s over American cultural attitudes toward death. See especially Elizabeth Kubler-Ross, *On Death and Dying* (New York: Macmillan, 1969); and Ernest Becker, *The Denial of Death* (New York: Free Press, 1973).

28. Susan Sontag, *Illness as Metaphor* (New York: Farrar, Straus, and Giroux, 1978), 64–67.

29. "Social Talk," in *Lives of a Cell*, 90. For Thomas's further discussion of language, see the essays entitled "Information," "On Various Words," and "Living Language." He also deals with matters of philology and linguistics in *The Medusa and the Snail*. See especially the essays entitled "On Etymons and Hybrids" and "Notes on Punctuation."

30. These publication figures were quoted in an 11 April 1986 letter from Thomas's Czech translator, Dr. Miroslav Holub, to the author.

31. Joyce Carol Oates, "Beyond Common Sense: *The Lives of a Cell*," *New York Times Book Review*, 26 May 1974, 2–3.

32. Ibid., 3.

33. John Updike, "A New Meliorism," *New Yorker* 50 (15 July 1974): 83–86.

34. Ibid., 86.

35. The NOVA program on Lewis Thomas, entitled "Notes on a Biology Watcher: A Film with Lewis Thomas," was produced in 1981. The projected eight-part public television series, "The Strangeness of Nature," which was to have been hosted by Thomas and sponsored by WGBH in Boston and WNET in New York, did not receive sufficient funding and was never produced.

36. Though the majority of these essays first appeared in the *New England Journal of Medicine* between May 1974 and August 1978, at least two pieces first appeared elsewhere. "Medical Lessons from History" appeared as "Biomedical Science and Human Health: The Long-Range Prospect" in *Daedalus* 106, no. 3 (Summer 1977): 163–71; and "The Youngest and

Brightest Thing Around" appeared in slightly different form as an op-ed piece in the *New York Times*, 2 July 1978, sec. E, 15.

37. Paul Gray, "In Celebration of Life," *Time* 113 (14 May 1979): 86–94.

38. "Why Montaigne Is Not a Bore," in *The Medusa and the Snail* (New York: Viking Press, 1979), 146.

39. "The Youngest and Brightest Thing Around," in *Medusa and the Snail*, 18.

40. "On Magic in Medicine," in *Medusa and the Snail*, 21.

41. "Medical Lessons from History," in *Medusa and the Snail*, 169.

42. "The Wonderful Mistake," in *Medusa and the Snail*, 30.

43. "The Selves," in *Medusa and the Snail*, 42.

44. "On Disease," in *Medusa and the Snail*, 99. Thomas also discusses his theory of disease in "A Meliorist View of Disease and Dying," *The Journal of Medicine and Philosophy*, 1, no. 3 (September 1976): 212–21. See especially p. 215.

45. This quote from E. O. Wilson's review of *The Medusa and the Snail* is reprinted on the dust jacket of Thomas's book.

46. Howard Nemerov points out this same connection in his essay "Lewis Thomas, Montaigne, and Human Happiness," in *New and Selected Essays* (Carbondale: Southern Illinois University Press, 1985), 223–31.

47. "Interview with Lewis Thomas," 19 October 1982, included in the appendix to Diane Dowdy, "Literary Science: A Rhetorical Analysis of an Essay Genre and Its Tradition" (Ph.D. diss., University of Wisconsin–Madison, 1984), 515.

48. Updike, "A New Meliorism," 84.

49. "On the Nature of Nature," in *In Celebration of the Joy of Science: Chandler Alton Stetson, 1921–1977* (New York: Josiah Macy, Jr., Foundation, 1980), 7–14. This passage appears on p. 10.

50. *Lives of a Cell*, 142.

Chapter Four

1. Jeremy Bernstein, "Science Education for the Non-Scientist," *American Scholar* 52 (Winter 1983): 10.

2. "Humanities and Science," in *Late Night Thoughts on Listening to Mahler's Ninth Symphony* (New York: Viking Press, 1983), 150.

3. "On the Uncertainty of Science," *Harvard Magazine* 83, no. 1 (September–October 1980): 19–22. This essay remains uncollected.

4. All of the proceedings from the NYU symposium "Infection, Immunity, and the Language of Cells: A Meeting in Honor of Lewis Thomas" were later collected and edited by H. Sherwood Lawrence in a special commemorative issue of *Cellular Immunology* 82, no. 1 (November 1983).

5. Lawrence, "Kober Medal."

6. "Thomas Becomes Princeton Building," *Princeton Weekly Bulletin,* 28 April 1986, 1.

7. "Oswald Avery and the Cascade of Surprises," *Esquire* 100 (December 1983): 74–78.

8. Erwin Chargaff, "A Quick Climb up Mount Olympus," *Science* 159 (29 March 1968): 1448.

9. Peter Medawar, *Pluto's Republic* (New York: Oxford University Press, 1982), 263.

10. See my interview with Lewis Thomas in the Appendix.

11. Paul Starr, *The Social Transformation of American Medicine* (New York: Basic Books, 1982).

12. See *Youngest Science,* 5.

13. Stephen Jay Gould, "Calling Dr. Thomas," *New York Review of Books* 30, no. 12 (21 July 1983): 12.

14. See "How to Fix the Premedical Curriculum," in *Medusa and the Snail,* 137–41.

15. Jeremy Bernstein, "A Doctor's Life," *New Yorker* 58 (14 February 1983): 111.

16. H. Sherwood Lawrence, "An Appreciation: Notes of a Lewis Thomas–Watcher," *Cellular Immunology* 82, no. 1 (November 1983): 139.

17. Ibid., 141. See also Thomas's essay "On the AIDS Problem," *Discover* 4 (May 1983): 42–47. The sudden outbreak of AIDS has made Thomas's earlier predictions in *The Youngest Science* about totally eliminating major infectious diseases sound uncomfortably like Lord Kelvin's confident predictions in the late nineteenth century about prenuclear physics having reached a full understanding of the universe. Thomas's article on AIDS offers a considerably less optimistic view of the struggle against infectious disease.

18. *Youngest Science,* 151–52.

19. The results of some elegant experiments based in part on Thomas's hypotheses have been reported in a recent issue of *Scientific American.* See Gary K. Beauchamp, Kunio Yamazaki, and Edward A. Boyse, "The Chemosensory Recognition of Genetic Individuality," *Scientific American* 253 (July 1985): 86–92.

20. See Ronald Bailey, "Politics of the Cell," *Commentary* 78 (September 1984): 72–74.

21. Jonathan Schell's *The Fate of the Earth,* which was published by Knopf in 1982, appeared in the *New Yorker* in three installments, on 1, 8, and 15 February 1983.

22. These articles are C. Holden, "Scientists Describe Nuclear Winter," *Science* 222 (18 November 1983): 822–23; R. P. Turco et al., "Nuclear Winter: Global Consequences of Multiple Nuclear Explosions," *Science* 222 (23 December 1983): 1283–92; and Paul R. Ehrlich et al., "Long-term Biological Consequences of Nuclear War," *Science* 222 (23 December 1983): 1293–1300.

23. Thomas's review first appeared as "Unacceptable Damage" in the *New York Review of Books,* 28, no. 14 (24 September 1981): 3.

24. "Late Night Thoughts on Listening to Mahler's Ninth Symphony," in *Late Night Thoughts,* 166.

25. Ibid., 168.

26. See Peter Medawar, *Advice to a Young Scientist* (New York: Harper and Row), 105–106.

27. Ibid., 102.

28. "Making Science Work," in *Late Night Thoughts,* 22.

29. Cited by Thomas in "Altruism," in *Late Night Thoughts,* 103. See also J. B. S. Haldane, *On Being the Right Size and Other Essays,* ed. John M. Smith (New York: Oxford University Press, 1985). R. D. Hamilton has also written on the genetic probabilities of altruistic behavior. See also Peter Dawkins, *The Selfish Gene* (New York: Oxford University Press, 1976).

30. "The Mimosa Girdler," *New England Journal of Medicine* 301 (29 November 1979): 1226.

31. Sir Arthur Conan Doyle, *The Annotated Sherlock Holmes,* edited with introduction, notes, and biography by William S. Baring-Gould (New York: Clarkson N. Potter, 1967), 1:154.

32. "Late Night Thoughts," 165.

33. See Leonard Bernstein, *The Unanswered Question: Six Talks at Harvard,* Charles Eliot Norton Lectures (Cambridge: Harvard University Press, 1976), chap. 5.

34. See "Scientific Frontiers and National Frontiers: A Look Ahead," *Foreign Affairs* 62 (Spring 1984): 966–94.

35. This was in fact the title of an excerpt from Thomas's Elihu Root lectures, published as "Are Altruism and Cooperation Natural?" in *Harpers* 269 (July 1984): 26–27.

36. "Scientific Frontiers," 984.

37. Ibid., 985.

38. Ibid., 988.

39. Ibid., 989–90.

40. "TTAPS for the Earth," *Discover* 5 (February 1984), 30–34. Thomas's essay is based on two articles published in *Science* in December 1983. See footnote 22 of this chapter.

41. Apparently these lectures remain unpublished. My comments are based on a typescript copy marked "Lipkin I–III" sent to me by Dr. Thomas's secretary. Lipkin III is entitled "The Puzzlement of Humans."

42. "Lipkin I," 18 [typescript copy].

43. Ibid., 2.

44. Ibid., 3–5.

45. "Scientific Frontiers," 989.

46. Thomas also discusses Bickerton's work with Hawaiian creole in "On Speaking of Speaking," in *Late Night Thoughts,* 49–54. See also Derek Bickerton, *Roots of Language* (Ann Arbor: Karoma, 1981).

47. See the editorial headnote for "TTAPS for the Earth," 30.

48. See Curt Covey, Stephen H. Schneider, and Starley L. Thompson, "Global Atmospheric Effects of Massive Smoke Injections from a Nuclear War: Results from General Circulation Model Simulations," *Nature* 308 (1 March 1984): 21–25.

49. Quoted in Barbara Delatiner, "Scientist's Poetry Blends with Art," *New York Times,* 30 September 1984, sec. 21, 19.

50. Delatiner speaks of fourteen poems in her interview, but Dr. Thomas's secretary sent me a typescript copy including only thirteen. The missing poem is "On Insects," which was published in the *New Yorker* 47 (10 July 1971): 28.

51. See the appendix to *The Youngest Science,* 249–61.

52. Thomas quotes these lines in "Lipkin II," 7–8. See also Julian of Norwich, *Revelations of Divine Love,* ed. Roger Roberts (Wilton, Ct: Morehouse-Barlow, 1982).

53. As quoted by Wallace A. Clyde, Jr., and Gerald W. Fernard, "Mycoplasmas: The Pathogens' Pathogens," *Cellular Immunology* 82, no. 1 (November 1983): 90.

Chapter Five

1. See Oliver Sacks, *Awakenings* (New York: Dutton, 1983), *A Leg to Stand On* (New York: Summit Books, 1984), and *The Man Who Mistook His Wife for a Hat and Other Clinical Tales* (New York: Summit Books, 1985); Richard Selzer, *Confessions of a Knife* (New York: Simon and Schuster, 1979), *Mortal Lessons: Notes on the Art of Surgery* (New York: Simon and Schuster, 1982), *Letters to a Young Doctor* (New York: Simon and Schuster, 1982), *Taking the World in for Repairs* (New York: Morrow, 1986), and *Rituals of Surgery* (New York: Morrow, 1987); Gerald Weissman, *The Woods Hole Cantata: Essays on Science and Society* (New York: Dodd, Mead & Co., 1985), and *They All Laughed at Christopher Columbus: Tales of Medicine and the Art of Discovery* (New York: Times Books, 1987); Harold J. Morowitz, *The Wine of Life: And Other Essays on Societies, Energy and Living Things* (Woodbridge, Ct: Ox Bow Press, 1979), *Mayonnaise and the Origin of Life: Thoughts of Mind and Molecules* (New York: Berkley Publishers, 1987), and *Cosmic Joy and Local Pain: Musings of a Mystic Scientist* (New York: Charles Scribner's Sons, 1987); and Milton J. Slocum, *Manhattan Country Doctor* (New York: Charles Scribner's Sons, 1986).

2. Quoted by Lady Jean Medawar at a memorial service for Sir Peter Medawar at New York University School of Medicine on 17 October 1987. Thomas reaffirmed many of these same sentiments in his own tribute to Medawar. For an abridged version of their remarks, see "In Memoriam Peter Medawar," *Scientist* 117 (25 January 1988): 13.

3. See Georg Lukács, "On the Nature and Form of the Essay," in *Soul and Form,* trans. Anna Bostock (Cambridge: MIT Press, 1974), 1–18.

Selected Bibliography

PRIMARY SOURCES

Books

Could I Ask You Something? New York: Library Fellows of the Whitney Museum of American Art, 1985. Poetry.

Late Night Thoughts on Listening to Mahler's Ninth Symphony. New York: Viking Press, 1983.

The Lives of a Cell: Notes of a Biology Watcher. New York: Viking Press, 1974.

The Medusa and the Snail: More Notes of a Biology Watcher. New York: Viking Press, 1979.

The Youngest Science: Notes of a Medicine-Watcher. New York: Viking Press, 1983. Memoir.

Articles and Essays

Before 1970, the bulk of Thomas's writing consisted of biomedical research articles published in medical and scientific journals. A prolific technical writer, Thomas has probably written over two hundred science articles. For reasons of space, I have not listed most of these medical articles because they are already compiled in a bibliography of Thomas's scientific publications included in the commemorative issue of *Cellular Immunology* honoring him. I have only listed those medical articles that seem to have a direct thematic bearing on his popular essay writing. For a complete listing of Thomas's medical publications, see the bibliography in *Cellular Immunology* 82, no. 1 (November 1983): 7–16.

Thomas sometimes reprinted the same essay in abridged form or with a different title, and I have tried to indicate all of these variants. The essay citations are listed alphabetically rather than chronologically for ease of indexing. His essay collections were almost entirely compiled of essays published previously, and he tended to do little editing or revision of an essay once it had appeared in print. A number of his recent essays in *Discover* have not yet appeared in book form and await a collected edition of his work.

"Adaptive Aspects of Inflammation." In *Immunopathology of Inflammation,* edited by Bernard K. Forscher and John C. Houck, 1–10. Excerpta Medica Congress Series no. 229. Amsterdam: Excerpta Medica, 1971.

126

"Advice to the Advisor." *Discover* 2 (September 1981): 58–59.

"Altruism." *New York Times Magazine,* 4 July 1976, 108–109. Also "Altruism: Self-Sacrifice for Others." *Saturday Evening Post* 254, 5 (May/June 1982): 42–45.

"Americans Are Fitter Than Ever but Obsessed with Health." *U.S. News and World Report* 88 (24 March 1980): 70–71. Interview.

"Antaeus in Manhattan." *New England Journal of Medicine* 286 (11 May 1972): 1046–47.

"Any Question Now Is Askable." *Science Digest* 87 (January 1980): 36–37.

"An Apology." *New England Journal of Medicine* 294 (13 May 1976): 1107–1108.

"Are Altruism and Cooperation Natural?" *Harpers* 269 (July 1984): 26–27.

"Are We Fit to Fit In?" *Sierra* 67 (March/April 1982): 49–52.

"An Argument for Cooperation." *Discover* 5 (August 1984): 66–69.

"The Art of Teaching Science." *New York Times Magazine,* 14 March 1982: 89–90.

"The Attic of the Brain." *Discover* 1 (November 1980): 32–33.

"Autonomy." *New England Journal of Medicine* 287 (13 July 1972): 90–92.

"Basic Medical Research: A Long-Term Investment." *Technical Review* 83 (May/June 1981): 42–44.

"Basic Science and American Business." *Bulletin of the New York Academy of Medicine,* 2d ser. 57 (July/August 1981): 493–502.

"Basic Science and the Pentagon." *Discover* 3 (April 1982): 58–62.

"Biomedical Science and Human Health: The Long-Range Prospect." *Daedalus* 106, no. 3 (Summer 1977): 163–71.

"Biostatistics in Medicine." *Science* 198 (18 November 1977): 675.

"Cancer Risk: Less Than We Fear." *Reader's Digest* 124 (February 1984): 142–43.

"Cancer's End." *Self* 5 (January 1983): 58–60.

"Cell Fusion: Does It Represent a Universal Urge to Join Up?" *Science Digest* 86 (December 1979): 52–54.

"Ceti." *New England Journal of Medicine* 286 (10 February 1972): 306–307.

"Computers." *New England Journal of Medicine* 288 (14 June 1973): 1288–89.

"Dark Secret of Doctors: Most Things Get Better by Themselves." *New York Times Magazine,* 4 July 1976, 108–109. Interview.

"The Deacon's Masterpiece." *New England Journal of Medicine* 292 (9 January 1975): 93–95.

"Death in the Open." *New England Journal of Medicine* 288 (11 January 1973): 92–93.

"Debating the Unknowable." *Atlantic Monthly* 124 (July 1981): 49–52.

"Diagnosing the Doctor." *Reader's Digest* 123 (November 1983): 185–88.

"A Doctor's Love Letter to Women." *Self* 5 (February 1983): 68.

"Dying as Failure." *Annals of the American Academy of Political and Social Sciences,* no. 447 (January 1980): 1–4.

"An Earnest Proposal." *New England Journal of Medicine* 285 (11 November 1971): 1132–33.

"Edges of Knowledge." *Science Digest* 84 (October 1978): 42–45.

"Enormous Party." *House and Garden* 149 (December 1977): 86–89.

"An Epidemic of Apprehension." *Discover* 4 (November 1983): 78–80.

"Facts of Life." *New England Journal of Medicine* 296 (23 June 1977): 1462–64.

"Falsity and Failure." *Discover* 2 (June 1981): 38–39.

"A Fear of Pheromones." *New England Journal of Medicine* 285 (12 August 1971): 392–93.

"From Lewis Thomas: Optimism on Solving Disease Riddles." *Science Digest* 85 (February 1979): 66–69.

"Future Impact of Science and Technology on Medicine." *Bioscience* 24 (February 1974): 99–105. Also in *Vital Speeches* 40 (15 November 1973): 75–80.

"The Future Place of Science in the Art of Healing." *Journal of Medical Education* 51, no. 1 (January 1976): 23–29.

"Future Prospects for Basic Science in Medicine." *Bulletin of the American Academy of Arts and Sciences* 34, no. 1 (October 1980): 20–41.

"Germs." *New England Journal of Medicine* 287 (14 September 1972): 553–55.

"Getting at the Roots of a Deep Puzzle." *Discover* 7 (March 1986): 65–66.

"Getting the Grip on the Grippe." *Discover* 2 (January 1981): 46–47.

"Guessing and Knowing: Reflections on the Science and Technology of Medicine." *Saturday Review of Science* 55 (23 December 1972): 52–57. Excerpt from address.

"Has Medical Science Reached the End of the Road? Not by a Long Shot." *Modern Medicine* 44 (1 December 1976): 38–51.

"The Hazards of Science." *New England Journal of Medicine* 296 (10 February 1977): 324–28. Also reprinted in *Science Digest* 81 (March 1977): 71.

"The Health-Care System." *New England Journal of Medicine* 293 (11 December 1975): 1245–46.

"Heroin." *New England Journal of Medicine* 286 (9 March 1972): 531–33.

"Hopeful Prophet Who Speaks for Human Aspirations." *Smithsonian* 11 (April 1980): 127–128. Interview.

"How Doctors Have Lost Touch." *McCall's* 110 (November 1982): 210.

"How Should Humans Pay Their Way?" *New York Times*, 24 August 1981, sec. A, 15.

"How to Fix the Premedical Curriculum." *New England Journal of Medicine* 298 (25 May 1978): 1180–81.

"Hybris in Science?" *Science* 200 (30 June 1978): 1459–62.

"The Iks." *New England Journal of Medicine* 288 (10 May 1973): 1009–1010.

"Information." *New England Journal of Medicine* 287 (14 December 1972): 1238–39.

"The Limitations of Medicine as a Science." In *The Manipulation of Life,* edited by Robert Esbjornson, 1–21. San Francisco: Harper and Row, 1984.

"The Lives of a Cell." *New England Journal of Medicine* 284 (13 May 1971): 1082–83.

"Living Language." *New England Journal of Medicine* 289 (13 December 1973): 1298–1300.

"The Long Habit." *New England Journal of Medicine* 286 (13 April 1972): 825–26.

"Magic in Medicine: It's More Than Good Health Habits." *Science Digest* 86 (October 1979): 16–19. Excerpt.

"Making Science Work." *Discover* 2 (March 1981): 88–89. Also in *Saturday Evening Post* 256, 8 (November 1984): 36–40.

"Man's Role on Earth." *New York Times Magazine,* 1 April 1984, 36–37.

"Marine Models in Modern Medicine." *Oceanus* 19, no. 2 (Winter 1976): 2–5.

"The MBL." *New England Journal of Medicine* 286 (8 June 1972): 1254–56.

"Medicine Needs More Research, Not More 'Caring.' " *Discover* 6 (September 1985): 85–87.

"Medicine without Science." *Atlantic Monthly* 247 (April 1981): 40–42.

"Medicine's New Role." *Discover* 5 (December 1984): 24–25.

"Medicine's Second Revolution." *Science 84,* 5 (November 1984): 93–95.

"The Medusa and the Snail." *New England Journal of Medicine* 296 (12 May 1977): 1103–1105.

"A Meliorist View of Disease and Dying." *Journal of Medicine and Philosophy* 1 (September 1976): 212–21.

"The Mimosa Girdler." *New England Journal of Medicine* 301 (29 November 1979): 1224–26.

"The Music of *This* Sphere." *New England Journal of Medicine* 285 (14 October 1971): 904–906.

"Natural Man." *New England Journal of Medicine* 288 (12 April 1973): 779–80.

"Natural Science." *New England Journal of Medicine* 288 (8 February 1973): 307–308. Also in *Science* 179 (30 March 1973): 1283.

"Note from a Universe-Watcher: 'We Are the Newest, the Youngest, and the Brightest Thing Around.' " *New York Times,* 2 July 1978, sec. E, 15. Reprinted as "We Are the Youngest and Brightest Things in Nature." *Self* 1 (May 1979): 62–64.

"Notes of a Biology Watcher." *Harper's* 246 (February 1973): 98–99. Reprint.

"Nuclear Winter, Again." *Discover* 5 (October 1984): 57–58.

"On Alchemy." *Discover* 3 (May 1982): 34–35.

"On Altruism." *Discover* 3 (March 1982): 58–59.

"On Ants and Us." *Discover* 2 (February 1981): 52–53.

"On Artificial Intelligence." *New England Journal of Medicine* 302 (28 February 1980): 506–508.

"On Basic Research." *Discover* 2 (January 1981): 42–43.

"On Bewilderment." *Discover* 2 (July 1981): 42–43, 47.

"On Clever Animals." *Discover* 3 (September 1982): 58–59.

"On Cloning a Human Being." *New England Journal of Medicine* 291 (12 December 1974): 1296–97.

"On Committees." *New England Journal of Medicine* 294 (12 February 1976): 384–85.

"On Etymons and Hybrids." *New England Journal of Medicine* 290 (9 May 1974): 1069–70.

"On Global Habitability and NASA." *Discover* 4 (June 1983): 65–66.

"On Good Health." *Vogue* 169 (June 1979): 200–201.

"On Life in a Hell of a Place." *Discover* 4 (October 1983): 42–45.

"On Magic in Medicine." *New England Journal of Medicine* 299 (31 August 1978): 461–63.

"On Mahler's Ninth Symphony." *Discover* 3 (November 1982): 69–70.

"On Meddling." *New England Journal of Medicine* 294 (11 March 1976): 599–600.

"On Medicine and the Bomb." *Discover* 2 (October 1981): 32–33.

"On My Magical Metronome." *Discover* 4 (January 1983): 58–59.

"On Natural Death." *Blair and Ketchums* 6 (May 1979): 47. Excerpt.

"On Nursing." *Discover* 3 (June 1982): 58–59.

"On Probability and Possibility." *New England Journal of Medicine* 290 (14 February 1974): 388–89.

"On Science and 'Science.' " *Discover* 3 (August 1982): 64–65.

"On Science and Uncertainty." *Discover* 1 (October 1980): 58–59.

"On Science Business." *New England Journal of Medicine* 302 (17 January 1980): 157–58.

"On Smell." *New England Journal of Medicine* 302 (27 March 1980): 731–33.

"On Societies as Organisms." *New England Journal of Medicine* 285 (8 July 1971): 101–102.

"On the AIDS Problem." *Discover* 4 (May 1983): 42–47.

"On the Nature of Cooperation." *Discover* 2 (November 1981): 58–59.

"On the Nature of Nature." In *In Celebration of the Joy in Science: Chandler Alton Stetson, 1921–1977,* 7–14. New York: Josiah Macy, Jr., Foundation, 1980.

"On the Need for Asylums." *Discover* 2 (December 1981): 68–69.

"On the Problem of Dementia." *Discover* 2 (August 1981): 34–35.

"On the Science and Technology of Medicine." *Daedalus* 106, no. 1 (Winter 1977): 35–46. Reprinted in *Doing Better and Feeling Worse: Health in the United States,* edited by J. H. Knowles, 35–46. New York: Norton, 1977.

"On Transcendental Metaworry (TMW)." *New England Journal of Medicine* 291 (10 October 1974): 779–80.

"On Various Words." *New England Journal of Medicine* 289 (8 November 1973): 1024–26.

"On Yellow Rain and Science." *Discover* 4 (August 1983): 80–82.

"One Man's Candidates for the Wonders of the World." *New York Times,* 7 June 1983, sec. C, 1. Reprinted as "Seven True Wonders of the World." *Reader's Digest* 124 (April 1984): 130–33.

"Organelles as Organisms." *New England Journal of Medicine* 287 (10 August 1972): 294–95.

"Oswald Avery and the Cascade of Surprises." *Esquire* 100 (December 1983): 74–76.

"Peering at a Microbial World: Germs Are Not Our Enemy." *Science Digest* 86 (November 1979): 30–35. Excerpt.

"The Planning of Science." *New England Journal of Medicine* 289 (12 July 1973): 89–90.

"Ponds." *New England Journal of Medicine* 298 (27 April 1978): 954–55.

"Premedical and Preclinical Education: Prospects for Fusion." *Bulletin of the New York Academy of Medicine,* 2d ser. 49, no. 4 (April 1973): 272–79.

"Scientific Frontiers and National Frontiers: A Look Ahead." *Foreign Affairs* 62 (Spring 1984): 966–94.

"The Selves." *New England Journal of Medicine* 299 (27 July 1978): 185.

"Sky Reporter." *Natural History* 84 (February 1975): 12–13.

"Social Talk." *New England Journal of Medicine* 287 (9 November 1972): 973–75.

"Some Biomythology." *New England Journal of Medicine* 289 (9 August 1973): 309–311.

"Speaking of Speaking." *Discover* 4 (March 1983): 80–81.

"The Strangeness of Nature." *New England Journal of Medicine* 298 (29 June 1978): 1454–56.

"The Technology of Medicine." *New England Journal of Medicine* 285 (9 December 1971): 1366–68.

"Thoughts of a Countdown." *New England Journal of Medicine* 284 (10 June 1971): 1311–12.

"To Err Is Human." *New England Journal of Medicine* 294 (8 January 1976): 99–100.

"To Tell the Truth." *Discover* 1 (December 1980): 54–55.

"To the Computers of Destruction: Do Nothing 'Till You Hear from Me." *Psychology Today* 8 (July 1984): 72–73. Excerpt.

"TTAPS for the Earth." *Discover* 5 (February 1984): 30–34.

"The Tucson Zoo." *New England Journal of Medicine* 296 (14 April 1977): 863–64.

"Unacceptable Damage." *New York Review of Books* 28 (24 September 1981): 3.

"Unhealthy Obsession." *Duns Review* 107 (June 1976): 81–82. Reprint.
"Vibes." *New England Journal of Medicine* 286 (13 January 1972): 88–90.
"View from the Corner of the Eye." *Discover* 2 (April 1981): 68–69.
"Warts, Brains, and Other Astonishments." *Reader's Digest* 115 (October 1979): 97–100. Excerpt.
"We're a Nation of Long-Lived Hypochondriacs." *Forbes* 122 (4 September 1978): 22–23.
"What a Way to Go." *Reader's Digest* 116 (June 1980): 205–206. Excerpt.
"What Doctors Don't Know." *New York Review of Books* 34, no. 14 (24 September 1987): 6–11.
"When Outer Space Speaks." *Reader's Digest* 111 (July 1977): 181–82.
"Who Will Be Saved? Who Will Pay the Cost?" *Discover* 4 (February 1983): 30–32.
"Why Can't Computers Be More Like Us?" *Saturday Evening Post* 248 (October 1976): 8.
"Why Two Cells Fuse." *Newsweek* 94 (20 August 1979): 50–51.
"The World's Biggest Membrane." *New England Journal of Medicine* 289 (13 September 1973): 376–77.
"Your Very Good Health." *New England Journal of Medicine* 287 (12 October 1972): 761–62.

Miscellaneous Prose and Introductions to Other Works

Foreword to *Sagittal Section: Poems New and Selected,* by Miroslav Holub. Translated by Stuart Friebert and Dana Habova. Field Translation Series no. 3. Oberlin: Oberlin College, 1980.
Foreword to *The Woods Hole Cantata: Essays on Science and Society,* by Gerald Weissman. New York: Dodd, Mead, & Co., 1985.
Foreword to *Natural Obsessions: The Search for the Oncogene,* by Natalie Angier. Boston: Houghton Mifflin, 1988.
Introduction to *The Search for Solutions,* by Horace Freeland Judson. New York: Holt, Rinehart and Winston, 1980.
The Lasker Awards: Four Decades of Scientific Medical Progress. New York: Raven Press, 1986.

Poetry

"Allen Street." [Harvard Medical School] *Aesculapiad* (1937): 81–83. Reprinted in *The Youngest Science,* 250–53.
"Design for Heaven." *Atlantic Monthly* 167 (April 1941): 502.
"Limitation." *Atlantic Monthly* 174 (October 1944): 119.
"Millennium." *Atlantic Monthly* 167 (May 1941): 636.
"My Brain." *Advances* 1, no. 4 (Fall 1984): 29.
"On Insects." *New Yorker* 47, no. 21 (10 July 1971): 28.

"Socialism for Beginners." *Saturday Evening Post* 214 (19 July 1941): 42. Signed "Thomas Lewis."
"Three Poems": "Ward Rounds," "Meditation—103 Fahrenheit," and "Plant a Metal Seed." *Hopkins Review* 1, no. 2 (Spring 1948): 38–41.
"Tombstone Inscription." *Atlantic Monthly* 168 (December 1941): 738.
"Vitamins." *Atlantic Monthly* 167 (March 1941): 372.
"Ward One." *Harper's Bazaar* 74 (October 1941): 138. Signed "Thomas Lewis."

Juvenilia

"Christmas Comes to the Jukes Family." *Princeton Tiger*, 14 December 1932, 16. Signed "L.T." Humorous prose sketch.
"Disrespectful Note on the Divine Plan." *Princeton Tiger*, 21 October 1932, 17. Signed "L.T." Poem.
"The Horror at Fuhrtbang." *Princeton Tiger*, 25 November 1931, 23. Signed "ELTIE." Humorous prose sketch.
"The Huddle." *Princeton Tiger*, 21 October 1931, 22. Signed "ELTIE." Humorous dramatic sketch.
"Like a Light." *Princeton Tiger*, 3 June 1931, 25. Signed "ELTIE." Humorous prose sketch.
"Princeton's Movie Industry." *Princeton Tiger*, 18 February 1931, 23. Signed "ELTIE." Humorous prose sketch.
"Reflections on the Evil of Drink." *Princeton Tiger*, 19 May 1932, 12. Signed "L.T." Poem.
"Reflections on the Investigation." *Princeton Tiger*, 28 April 1932, 15. Signed "L.T." Poem.
"Something New in Advertising." *Princeton Tiger*, 18 February 1931, 21. Signed "ELTIE." Humorous prose sketch.

SECONDARY SOURCES

Books and Tributes

Bernstein, Jeremy. *Experiencing Science: Profiles in Discovery.* New York: Basic Books, 1978. Chapter five, "Lewis Thomas: Life of a Biology Watcher," contains basically the same material originally published as a *New Yorker* "Profile" in 1978.
Lawrence, H. Sherwood, ed. "Commemorative Issue in Honor of Lewis Thomas." *Cellular Immunology* 82, no. 1 (November 1983). A collection of scientific and technical articles in honor of Thomas given at the conference "Infection, Immunity, and the Language of Cells: A Meeting in Honor of Lewis Thomas." Held at New York University Medical

Center, 22 November 1982. These tributes to Dr. Thomas were also
summarized in Lois Wingerson, "NYU Symposium Honors Dr. Lewis
Thomas," *NYU Physician* 39, no. 3 (Spring 1983): 20–30.

Critical Articles

Nemerov, Howard. "Lewis Thomas, Montaigne, and Human Happiness."
In *New and Selected Essays,* with an introduction by Kenneth Burke,
223–31. Carbondale: Southern Illinois University Press, 1985. Nemerov
points to the influence of Bach in Thomas's "contrapuntal" essay style
and discusses some of the parallels between Thomas's and Montaigne's
views of human nature.

Shiring, Joan. "Recommended: Lewis Thomas." *English Journal* 73, no. 8
(December 1984): 55–56. An Austin, Texas, high school English teacher
describes her success in teaching Thomas's essays as a way of appealing
to both science and humanities students.

Weiland, Steven. " 'A Tune Beyond Us, Yet Ourselves': Medical Science
and Lewis Thomas." *Michigan Quarterly Review* 24 (Spring 1985):
293–306. A detailed examination of Thomas's literary career and of
the major themes in his books and essays: the morality of science, the
essential unity of life, the genetic roots of language, and the creative
value of metaphor. Weiland discusses the influence of Montaigne's style
as a model for Thomas's essays and praises Thomas's outspoken stand
against nuclear proliferation.

Interviews and Articles About

"Back to the Future." *Architectural Record* 174 (August 1986): 104–113.
Karen D. Stein describes the controversial new $29 million molecular-
biology laboratory at Princeton University named after Lewis Thomas.
The interior laboratory space was deliberately designed to promote
collaboration and information exchange among an interdisciplinary group
of researchers.

"Daily Closeup: The 'Wildness of Science.' " *New York Post,* 22 February
1973. Barbara Yuncker provides a brief profile of Thomas's career on
the occasion of his being named president of Memorial Sloan-Kettering
Cancer Institute.

"The Lives of Dr. Thomas." *Princeton Alumni Weekly* (2 December 1978):
18, 29. In a profile subtitled "Seeing a Whole Greater Than Its Parts,"
Stephen R. Dujack discusses the continuities in Thomas's career, from
medical student to president of Sloan-Kettering.

"The Muse of Medicine." *Esquire* 101 (March 1984): 72–77. Perhaps the
most perceptive and useful extended interview with Thomas. David
Hellerstein presents a wide-ranging series of comments by Thomas on

his career and research interests and on the future of medicine as a science.

"Narcissus, Pogo, and Lew Thomas' Wager." *JAMA [Journal of the American Medical Association]* 245 (10 April 1981): 1450–54. Roger J. Bulger notes how Thomas's optimism about man's prospects is a welcome antidote to the narcissism and pessimism of our times.

"NYU Symposium Honors Dr. Lewis Thomas." *NYU Physician* 39, no. 3 (Spring 1983): 20–30. Lois Wingerson offers a useful summary of the professional tributes to Thomas by his former students and colleagues; these tributes were later included along with the scientific papers published in the Lewis Thomas commemorative issue of *Cellular Immunology* 82, no. 1 (November 1983).

"Presentation of the George M. Kober Medal to Lewis Thomas." *Transactions of the Association of American Physicians* 96 (1983): cxviii–cxxxiii. H. Sherwood Lawrence reviews Thomas's career on the occasion of his receiving the Kober Medal in 1983.

"Profiles: Biology Watcher." *New Yorker* 54 (2 January 1978): 27–46. Jeremy Bernstein presents a detailed and extensive biographical profile of Thomas's life and career; this profile was later reprinted as chapter five of *Experiencing Science.*

Reviews

Bernstein, Jeremy. "A Doctor's Life." *New Yorker* 58 (14 February 1983): 109–14. In this extended review of *The Youngest Science,* Bernstein reflects on the differences between his interview of Thomas in 1978 and Thomas's subsequent handling of much of the same information in his memoir.

Gaylin, William. "A Doctor on Healing." *New York Times Book Review,* 27 February 1983, 3, 16–17. In this mixed review of *The Youngest Science,* Gaylin complains of the lack of sufficient autobiographical material in Thomas's medical memoir.

Gould, Stephen Jay. "Biological Musings." *New York Times Book Review,* 6 May 1979, 1, 32–33. Gould questions the accuracy of Thomas's melioristic vision in *The Medusa and the Snail,* given the complexities and ambiguities of nature, yet he praises Thomas's vision and sense of wonder.

————. "Calling Dr. Thomas." *New York Review of Books* 30, no. 12 (12 July 1983): 12–13. Gould finds *The Youngest Science* in some respects an overly nostalgic book, but he praises Thomas's understanding of the tradeoffs in modern medicine between personal patient care and high-tech efficiency.

Gray, Paul. "In Celebration of Life." *Time* 113 (14 May 1979): 86–94. A feature article containing a detailed overview of Thomas's career and an appreciative review of *The Medusa and the Snail.*

Klaw, Spencer. "A Celebrant of Life on Earth." *Natural History* 88 (June/July 1979): 98–102. Praise for the celebration of wonder and delight in *The Medusa and the Snail,* especially for Thomas's "perfectly controlled fusion of metaphor and fact."

Morgan, Ted. "Is There a Doctor in the House?" *Saturday Review* 6 (4 August 1979): 53–56. Morgan prefers the "plain and exact writing" of Thomas's *Medusa and the Snail* to the "overblown pastiche of 17th century prose" of the essays in Richard Selzer's *Confessions of a Knife.*

Oates, Joyce Carol. "Beyond Common Sense: *The Lives of a Cell.*" *New York Times Book Review,* 26 May 1974, 2–3. A perceptive and influential review of Thomas's first essay collection; Oates values his combination of graceful style and scientific rigor and praises his vision of the mystical interrelatedness of all life on earth.

Rabin, David. "Physician Heal Thyself: Thomas, Starr, and the Doctor-Patient Relationship." *Southern Medical Journal* 76 (November 1983): 1337–38. Rabin contrasts two views of the history and growth of American medicine and comments on the growing loss of confidence in the medical profession and the increasingly negative view of the physician as American medicine has changed from an art, as Thomas depicts his father's practice in *The Youngest Science,* to an increasingly impersonal science.

Updike, John. "Books: A New Meliorism." *New Yorker* 50 (15 July 1974): 83–86. Updike praises both the way in which the essays in *The Lives of a Cell* are unified by the theme of symbiosis and Thomas's "shimmering vision of a 'fusion around the earth'" that will spring from man's attempts to understand and communicate more information about the world in which he lives.

Dissertations

Dowdy, Diane. "Literary Science: A Rhetorical Analysis of an Essay Genre and Its Tradition." Ph.D. diss., University of Wisconsin–Madison, 1984. A valuable genre study of the scientific essay. Includes an interview with Lewis Thomas in the appendix.

White, Laurie L. "Modern Traditions of the Essay." Ph.D. diss., University of North Carolina–Greensboro, 1987. An innovative theoretical study of the modern essay, examining its rhetorical form in terms of Beale's theory of pragmatic discourse. Includes a useful analysis of Thomas's rhetorical style and technique.

Index